S0-BXX-246

Scythians

Black Sea

Byzantium

Asia Minor

Pergamum

Delphi

Athens

Olympia

Corinth

Sparta

yracuse

Knossos

Crete

Sidon

Tyre

Jerusalem

PROPERTY OF:
HEBREW DAY SCHOOL
OF CENTRAL FLORIDA

Alexandria

Memphis

Egypt

Series director: Michel Pierre, Professor of History
Art director: Giampiero Caiti
Assistant art director: Jean-Marie Mornard
Editor: Martine Prosper
American project editor: Joanne Fink
English text consultant: Walter O. Moeller,
  Senior Professor, Temple University.

The publisher would like to thank the following organizations for
their assistance in the preparation of this book: The Lebanese
office of Tourism, Paris; The Department of Research for
Underwater Archaeology (D.R.A.S.M., Marseille).

Library of Congress Cataloging-in-Publication Data

Adam, Jean-Pierre, 1937-
    Mediterranean civilizations.

    (The Human story)
    Translation of: La Méditerranée.
    Includes index.
    Summary: Describes the civilizations of the Mediterranean
region from the Mycenae in 1400 B.C. to the collapse of the
Byzantium empire in 1453. Focuses on the cultures of Ancient
Greece and Rome.
    1. Mediterranean Region—Civilization—Juvenile literature. [1.
Mediterranean Region—Civilization. 2. Civilization, Ancient. 3.
Greece—Civilization—To 146 B.C. 4. Rome—Civilization]   I.
Welply, Michaël, ill. II. Title. III. Series: Histoire des hommes.
English.
DE59.A3313 1987   909′.09822   86–42655
ISBN 0–382–09215–5

© 1985 by Casterman, originally published in French under the
Title *L'Histoire des Hommes: La Mediterranee*.
© 1987 English text, Silver Burdett Press.

Published pursuant to an agreement with Casterman, Paris.

First published in the United States in 1987
by Silver Burdett Press, Morristown, New Jersey.

All rights reserved.

Photographic Credits
Michel Pierre: pages 10, 11 18L, 32, 35, 38, 39, 43, 50R, 52, 53, 54,
55, 56, 57, 62, 63, 64, 65, 67, 68, 68, 71, 72, 75, 76. Jean-Pierre
Adam: pages 12, 22, 30, 34, 40, 50R, 58 60, 61, 63. Novosty: pages
44, 45. Giraudon: pages 18R, 21. Artephot/Trela: page 42.
Artephot/Nimattallah: pages 74, 75. Fulvio Roiter/Lebanese office
of Tourism: pages 14/15. D.R.A.S.M.: page 73.

THE HUMAN STORY
MEDITERRANEAN CIVILIZATIONS

Jean-Pierre Adam
English translation by Anthea Ridett
Illustrations by Michaël Welply

Silver Burdett Press
Morristown, New Jersey

CONTENTS

PREFACE

Today only a skeleton remains of the beauties of the ancient Mediterranean world. All that survives of twenty centuries of glory are the columns, capitals, pediments, and funeral stelae that rise from the ruins like bones whitened in the sun. Artists once decorated the temples in brilliant, almost gaudy hues, but we think of them as gleaming white, for their vivid colors have long since faded away.

In the depths of the sea lie the last fragments of the ships of Crete, Phoenicia, Carthage, Greece, and Rome, sunk by tempests or wrecked on hazardous reefs. Some of their cargoes have been recovered by archaeologists, reminders of the thousands of ships that once sailed regularly from Spain to Asia Minor, from Greece to the Nile Delta, and from the Near East to North Africa.

Even the landscape has changed radically since the days of Homer and Alexander. Twenty-five centuries ago the shores of the Mediterranean were far more heavily wooded than they are today. Generations of people have destroyed the forests, taking the wood to use as fuel and to build their houses or boats.

The scrubland typical of the Mediterranean area today is like a scar left by the great forests of ancient times. It is surprising to discover how many trees and plants that are considered indigenous to the area are in fact comparative newcomers. The ancient Greeks and Romans were introduced to lemons late in the development of their civilizations, and they never grew oranges, tomatoes, cacti, and aloes, which grew in America; or even eucalyptus, which originated in Australia. But the past is still there to remind us of Homer's tales, of the travels of Dido, of the long marches of the Roman legions, and of the Byzantine fleet. It is their memory, preserved in marble, in pottery, and in written texts, that will be recaptured in the pages of this book.

THE SEA IN THE MIDDLE OF LAND

Mediterraneum mare, "the sea in the midst of lands," was the Roman name for the interior sea that was the center of one of the greatest empires ever to exist. The Mediterranean is a huge lake lying between Africa, Asia, and Europe. It stretches from Gibraltar to the coast of Syria and covers nearly 970,000 square miles. To the navigators of old who sailed boldly across it or more safely along its coasts, it offered a variety of warm and sunlit landscapes. But the blue sky for which it is famous can be deceptive; a change of wind can easily turn the shining waters into violent waves. The different winds have been given a variety of local names—the Meltemi or Eltesian winds, the Tramonto, Sirocco, Mistral, and Ponente. The hero Ulysses, king of Ithaca, was powerless against the wrath of Aeolian winds that his companions let loose.

The Mediterranean coasts were rocky and jagged around the Aegean Sea, sandy and flat in North Africa, and covered by dense forest in Asia Minor and Gaul. As the centuries went by, prehistoric canoes landed on all these shores. Canoes were followed by small sailing ships in search of new harbors, new centers of trade, or new places to colonize. Guided by the stars, the first trading vessels carried in their holds the riches of one country to be bartered for those of another. They exchanged small objects, too, and words and ideas. Copper left Cyprus to feed the kilns of Greek and Asian bronzesmiths. Great beams of wood from Syria headed for Egypt; fine Greek ceramics were sold in Spain, which in turn exported lead. Thousands of jars of olive oil and wine reached the coast of Gaul where furs, salted goods, and slaves waited to make the return journey.

It was the Mediterranean that enabled the culture of Crete to grow and that protected the island from invasion by barbarians, who were frightened of the ocean. It was this "wine-dark" sea that opened up new horizons to the Phoenicians, a small nation surrounded on land by the Hittites, Mesopotamians, and Egyptians; it lured the Phoenicians with the mystery of strange far-off lands and the thrill of exploring the unknown. Phoenician traders exported the alphabet with their merchandise and spread their remarkable inventions wherever they went. Though they were subject to the powers that surrounded and later annexed them, the Phoenicians preserved the secrets of their sailing skills. It is said that one of the pharaohs ordered them to make the very first voyage around Africa.

Natural successors to the Phoenicians were the Greeks, Etruscans, and Carthaginians, who shared or competed with each other for trade and military power from the Aegean Sea to the Pillars of Hercules (Strait of Gibraltar), beyond which the huge ocean lay in wait for vessels bold enough to venture.

Then came Rome, and the Mediterranean became a Roman sea. The last pirates were subdued, and finally large trading vessels could carry their cargoes of wheat, oil, and wine in peace. The Romans were certain now of finding welcoming harbors and new cargoes, with nothing to fear but Neptune's stormy moods.

MINOS'S ISLE

The island of Crete rises from the waves in the center of the eastern Mediterranean, halfway between Greece and Egypt, and between Spain and Asia Minor. The waters around it are often disturbed by violent storms, and there have been many earthquakes in the region. Nevertheless, in Neolithic times, people came from the mainland and settled on Crete's coasts and plains. They grew wheat, vines, and olives in its rich soil and herded sheep on its hills and lower mountain slopes.

The early Cretans engaged in fishing and trading as well as agriculture. Their well-built boats created links with Egypt, Syria, Asia Minor, and Greece. They had three types of vessels: trading ships with square sails, manned by four to six sailors; lightweight galleys; and heavier galleys, with forty oarsmen, that could carry some fifteen passengers. The ships of Crete exported fruit, oil, fabrics, and bronze throughout the Aegean Sea, the Near East, and the Nile region.

As a mark of their wealth, the Cretans built large palaces, impressive royal residences at Mallia, Phaistos, Knossos, and Kato Zakro. The priest-kings who lived in them governed the island and were probably given the title *Minos*. Later, King Minos entered mythology as the son of Zeus and Europa, placed on the throne by the sea god Poseidon.

For centuries the Cretans dominated the whole Mediterranean; they made expeditions to the Greek mainland and established their power over the Aegean Sea. But around 1400 B.C. the Minoan civilization vanished. It was probably wiped out by an earthquake—one had already destroyed its palaces three hundred years earlier—and by invaders from Greece.

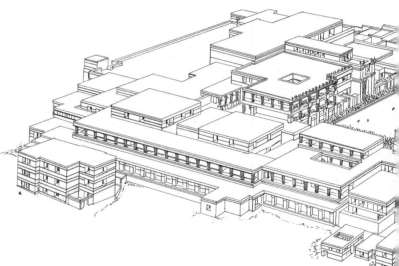

THE PALACE OF KNOSSOS

At the height of the Minoan civilization, the Palace of Knossos contained over thirteen hundred rooms, which were up to five stories high and served by a vast number of corridors. The masonry was simple, consisting of stone blocks and clay mortar, and the roof was flat, supported on rows of beams. To give the palace a luxurious look, the walls were decorated with frescoes. The floors were paved with gypsum tiles. The red-painted pillars were made of wood, set on stone bases, and topped by capitals shaped like wide rings.

Like the serpent, the bull was a symbol of fertility. In Crete, ceremonies were held in which young men and women took part in acrobatic exercises with an enraged bull. These games, which had a religious significance, were probably followed by the sacrifice of the bull, whose blood would symbolize the fertilization of the soil. These religious practices and the mazelike layout of the Cretan palaces gave rise to the legend of the terrible Minotaur—half man, half bull—who lived at the center of a labyrinth, or maze, and devoured young people. The myth was also based on the fact that the Minoans exacted tribute from people on the Greek mainland and made periodic raids there. The triumph of Theseus, who defeated the Minotaur, symbolized the Greek conquest of Crete in the Mycenaean period.

Crete, island of priest-kings and labyrinthine palaces.

In the palace precincts archaeologists have dug up huge storerooms containing piles of pithoi, *large urns in which oil, wine, and grain were kept. The agricultural wealth of Crete, shown by these stores, and the demands of trade encouraged the invention and development of writing; examples have been preserved on thousands of clay tablets. Some of the writings have been deciphered—one gives a list of Cretan shepherds around 1500 B.C.—but the scripts used on others are still a complete mystery.*

MYCENAE

In the second century A.D., the Greek historian Pausanias wrote of Mycenae: ''Little remains of it today, apart from a few ruined walls and the entrance gate of the citadel decorated with a relief sculpture of lionesses; it is said that the walls were built by a race of Cyclopes [one-eyed giants]. . . . At Tiryns all that remains are the walls, also built by the Cyclopes. The walls are made of stones so huge that two mules would not be able to move the smallest one.''

The ruins that so impressed Pausanias still make an impact today, evoking the memory of the Mycenaean people, who built these gigantic fortresses nearly thirty-three centuries ago, around 1400 B.C. They are symbols of a culture that had to defend itself against frequent invasions. But the Mycenaeans were also conquerors, and bands of soldiers often passed through the Lions' Gate at Mycenae, led by kings and generals clad in bronze or copper armor.

The peasants and artisans lived outside and around the citadel in houses made of clay and timber. The king's residence was built at the heart of the fortifications. Mycenaean palaces were much more crudely constructed than were those of Crete. They were centered on a *megaron*, a great hall entered through a pillared porch. The roof was held up by four pillars around a central hearth, with an opening in it, which served as a chimney.

In the fourteenth century B.C., the Mycenaeans were building monumental fortresses and defensive walls, and burying their kings in large circular tombs built into the sides of hills.

Two centuries later the Mycenaean civilization declined, when a severe and extended drought caused the rulers, fighters, and other leaders to emigrate in search of new lands. This left the Greek peninsula open to invasion and occupation by the Mycenaean Greeks' northern neighbors, the Dorian Greeks.

During his excavation of Mycenae, Heinrich Schliemann discovered six graves containing nineteen bodies, some with their faces covered by masks made from gold. The masks were fashioned on the actual faces of the dead, preserving their features for all eternity.

THE LION GATE

The ramparts around citadels were built to protect the royal residences, but in times of danger the people of the town and countryside could take refuge inside these walls. They are incredibly thick; built in a period when siege weapons consisted of arrows, javelins, and slings, their enormous size seems quite out of proportion. But the walls were intended to produce a psychological effect; anyone who went there with evil intentions was meant to see these colossal ramparts as a statement of superhuman, invincible power.

Golden masks in stone tombs; military parades beneath gigantic walls.

In the thirteenth century B.C., following a military expedition aimed at capturing the Dardanelles, a strait that separates Europe from Asia, the Mycenaeans entered forever into legend when they besieged and captured the city of Troy. The superb account of this exploit was passed down orally for generations, until the poet Homer wrote it down, around 800 B.C., in the form of two epic poems, the Iliad *(from Ilion, another name for Troy) and the* Odyssey *(from Odysseus, the Greek name for Ulysses). In the last century a German scholar, Heinrich Schliemann, who was fascinated by Homer's epics, excavated the sites of Troy and Mycenae. It was there, within the fortified walls, that he found the famous "circle graves" and dug up five royal tombs that contained skeletons covered in jewels and wearing gold masks. Schliemann believed he had discovered King Agamemnon and his companions; in fact, he was several centuries off the mark. The tombs were from the sixteenth century B.C., three hundred years before the siege of Troy.*

THE PHOENICIANS

Toward the end of the eleventh century B.C., the Mycenean culture was brought to an end by major civil and military disturbances. The way was open for the Phoenicians to become sole masters of the Mediterranean for several centuries. Their position between the two wealthiest regions of ancient times, Egypt and Mesopotamia, gave the Phoenicians an enormous economic advantage. They exported wine, wheat, and oil; cedarwood from their mountains; and large quantities of purple dye from their shores. They were the first people to discover the special properties of the murex, a shellfish that was found in abundance on their shores. Legend has it that a shepherd's dog, hunting for food, cracked a murex shell and released the red fluid it contained. Those present, struck by the bright color staining the dog's jaws, eagerly began collecting the ''purple'' of the murex to dye their fabrics.

The Phoenicians sailed from port to port along the coasts. They sought out profitable harbors and founded trading stations where they could anchor their ships, carry out repairs, and trade with the local people. In the eighth century B.C., they began to establish ports in Libya, Malta, Sicily, Sardinia, the Balearic Islands, Spain, Morocco, and Tunisia. Since money did not yet exist, Phoenician commerce was based on barter. Herodotus tells us that they produced large quantities of cheap goods imitating foreign art objects, which they used as a means of exchange. But at the same time, they had other industries with a reputation for quality: boatbuilding, woodworking, goldworking, and glass making. Moreover, although almost nothing remains of Phoenician architecture, apart from some tombs and defensive walls, their architects were famous; King Solomon called on them for the building of the temple in Jerusalem.

The great Phoenician cities were ports: Byblos (the oldest), Berytus, Tyre, and Sidon. All four are in what is now Lebanon. There the Phoenicians loaded their ships with purple dye, cedarwood, glass, copper, and bronze. On the coasts of Asia Minor, they obtained supplies of slaves, and in Arabia and Egypt they acquired incense, myrrh, and flax. Protected by their gods El and Baal and by their goddess Astarte, the Phoenicians sailed along the Mediterranean coasts as far away as Morocco and Spain. Their boats were designed for long voyages; made of cedarwood and pine, they were very strong. The boats had big square sails woven from Egyptian flax and were steered by two large oars fixed to the stern.

THE GLORY OF TYRE

During archaeological excavations at Byblos, hundreds of bronze figures with conical head-dresses and covered in gold leaf were found. The fine quality of the work and the wealth of gold attest to the splendor of the Phoenician ports. They are mentioned in the Bible by the prophet Ezekiel. Speaking of the port of Tyre, Ezekiel said, ''O thou that art situated at the entry of the sea. . . . All the ships of the sea with their mariners were in thee to occupy thy merchandise. . . . When thy wares went forth out of the seas, thou fillest many people; thou didst enrich the kings of the earth with the multitude of thy riches and of thy merchandise.'' (Ezekiel, Chapter 27)

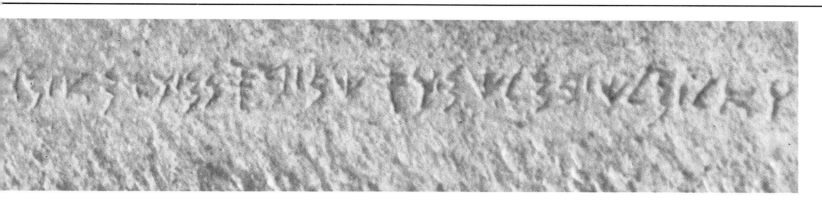

Until the end of the second millennium B.C., the people of the Near East knew of three great writing systems: Hittite hieroglyphics, which was used in Asia Minor; cuneiform, used in Syria, Mesopotamia, and Persia; and Egyptian hieroglyphics. They all took a long time to learn and to use; only the scribes were capable of using the three hundred cuneiform signs or the eight hundred Egyptian hieroglyphs. Around 1500 B.C. at Ugarit in northern Syria, the first alphabet was invented. It consisted of thirty characters, all consonants; the reader had to add the vowels mentally. This method was perfectly suitable for the phonetic structure of the Semitic languages and is still found today in the Hebrew and Arabic languages. Around 1000 B.C. the Phoenicians of Byblos, who were Canaanites, like the people of Ugarit, decided to make their alphabet even simpler by reducing it to twenty-two characters. The first known long text using this alphabet is a dedicatory inscription on the tomb of Ahiram, king of Byblos, who was buried early in the first millenium B.C.

Around 800 B.C. the Phoenician alphabet began to be adopted in the Greek world, where it gradually changed and was enriched by the addition of vowels. The following century, new characters were added to it in Italy, and it became the Latin alphabet that we still use today.

THE TWO
HARBORS OF CARTHAGE

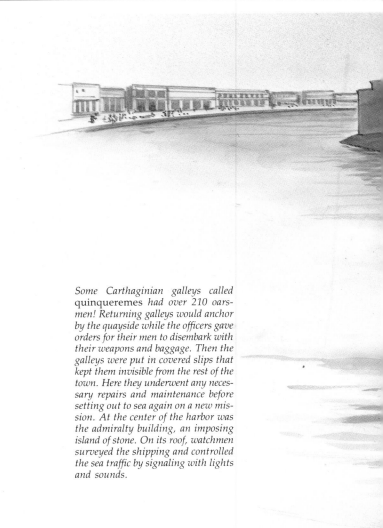

According to the Greek myth that the Roman poet Virgil took up in his *Aeneid*, Carthage was founded by a Phoenician princess—Elissa in the Greek texts, Dido in the Roman version. Her brother was Pygmalion, the cruel and ambitious king of Tyre. Pygmalion had had Elissa's husband Archabus murdered so that he could seize the husband's riches. Fearing for her life, the princess left Tyre and set sail toward the west with a small fleet. After visiting Cyprus, the fugitives landed in North Africa, near present-day Tunisia. The princess asked the local people to give her a plot of land where she might rest from the fatigues of her long voyage. They granted her "as much land as could be covered by a bull's hide." Elissa cunningly cut a bull's hide into narrow strips with which she encircled a huge piece of land. Here she built a citadel around which a new city grew which the Romans were to call *Carthago* ("Carthage"). Legend aside, archaeologists have since confirmed that the town was definitely founded by Phoenician colonists, in around 800 B.C.

Carthage stood on a large rocky promontory linked to the mainland by a strip of land. A horseshoe-shaped group of hills stood above the town to the west. On the highest hill rose the citadel of Byrsa, the final defense of the Carthaginians. From this height the whole town could be seen, with its two harbors linked by a canal; one harbor was reserved for trading vessels and the other for war ships.

Ships from all quarters of the Mediterranean jostled in the waters of the trading harbor. Some of them would be unloading gold, silver, iron, lead, copper, and tin, while others would be taking on board ivory, precious woods, cereals, and jars of oil.

Carthage became a great commercial center and founded its own trading colonies in North Africa, Sicily, southern Spain, and even Morocco. For a long time its possession of the Pillars of Hercules gave it control over access to the Atlantic Ocean.

Two great expeditions that went well beyond the Mediterranean were launched from Carthage. Himilco was sent with a small fleet to explore the west; he followed the Atlantic coast northward from the Iberian Peninsula to the British Isles, where tin and lead came from. The most famous voyage was made by Hanno, commander of an armada of sixty ships that he took down the west coast of Africa as far as the "Southern Horn," the Gulf of Guinea.

In the third century B.C., the ambitions of the proud city came into conflict with those of Rome. The two powers fought ferociously during the three Punic Wars. The first conflict (264 B.C.–241 B.C.) ended in a stalemate. During the second (218 B.C.–201 B.C.), Carthage was defeated, but it recovered. In 146 B.C., at the end of the Third Punic War, Carthage was destroyed, and its smoking ruins were strewn with salt, symbolic of sterility. Priests who came from Rome declared that the city was cursed forever. Nevertheless, under the Roman Empire, Carthage became a wealthy city again, with 300,000 inhabitants.

Some Carthaginian galleys called quinqueremes *had over 210 oarsmen! Returning galleys would anchor by the quayside while the officers gave orders for their men to disembark with their weapons and baggage. Then the galleys were put in covered slips that kept them invisible from the rest of the town. Here they underwent any necessary repairs and maintenance before setting out to sea again on a new mission. At the center of the harbor was the admiralty building, an imposing island of stone. On its roof, watchmen surveyed the shipping and controlled the sea traffic by signaling with lights and sounds.*

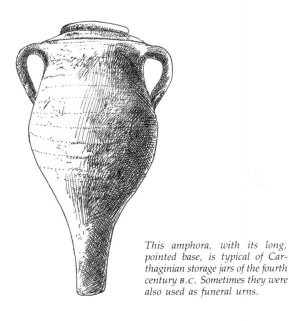

This amphora, with its long, pointed base, is typical of Carthaginian storage jars of the fourth century B.C. Sometimes they were also used as funeral urns.

Today the ancient harbors of Carthage look like small sanded-up pools squeezed among a few ruins and fine villas, whose gardens grow up the hill of Byrsa. It is hard to imagine that two thousand years ago the harbors were splendid symbols of Carthaginian power.

THE CITY OF CARTHAGE

In the third century B.C., Carthage was at the height of its power. It probably had a population of over 100,000, and almost all the Mediterranean peoples could be found there—Phoenicians, Numidians, Libyans, Iberians, and exiled Greeks. There were also a large number of slaves, mostly from Africa; sometimes they were freed and allowed to live in the city as free men.

The citizens of Carthage took an active role in politics. They elected a council of 104 magistrates, among whom were two *suffetes*, who governed together for a year. Generals were also elected by the citizens' assembly. They were answerable with their lives for the success of military operations: during the First Punic War, four generals were crucified for failing to defeat Rome! Generals always came from the aristocratic ruling class of Carthage. They commanded mercenaries, professional soldiers from all corners of the Mediterranean, who were united by greed for gain and the prestige of their leader, rather than by national pride, like the Macedonians and Romans.

Excavations at Carthage, at a site on the tip of Cape Bon near Tunis, have provided a great deal of information about daily life there. The richest Carthaginians lived in spacious villas, which stood along paved roads equipped with drains. The less well-off lived in tall apartment houses, often six stories high. Crowded together with only narrow alleys between them, these ''skyscrapers'' of antiquity were serious fire hazards; Carthage suffered two major fires.

The town was surrounded by rich farmland, which the Punic farmers tilled with an expertise admired by all the peoples of antiquity. One great landowner called Mago wrote a twenty-eight volume *Treatise on Agriculture*. It was so famous that when the Romans burned down the city's library in 146 B.C., they saved this treatise from the flames.

Some terra-cotta models of hip baths like this one have been found in the excavation of Carthage. Sometimes the models show people sitting in the baths and using a bowl to pour water over themselves.

Hannibal, son of Hamilcar Barca, belonged to one of the great aristocratic families of Carthage. Born around 247 B.C., he was brought up to hate the Romans, and as a young boy accompanied his father in the conquest of Spain. Hannibal became commander in chief and soon demonstrated his remarkable strategic skills. After crossing the Alps at the head of his army and elephants of war, he inflicted a major defeat on the Romans. But Hannibal was not able to present a serious threat to Rome, even after his great victory at Cannae in Apulia in 216 B.C. While he was waiting for reinforcements, which never came, he was unable to hold back the Romans, who renewed their offensive and landed in Africa. After a defeat at the battle of Zama in 202 B.C., Hannibal had to accept the humiliating peace terms imposed by Rome. Elected a suffete, he tried to get his revenge, but he was betrayed and fled east to the court of the king of Bithynia. There he was besieged, and in 182 B.C. he committed suicide rather than surrender to the Romans.

CHILD SACRIFICE

Like other peoples in antiquity, the Carthaginians sacrificed young children; this was called the Moloch in honor of their god Baal-Hammon, the ''master of heat,'' lord of the sun and of sacrificial fire. The ashes would be placed in an urn, which was then buried under a stone monument, often a small obelisk; archaeologists have found thousands of these urns. However, there were several ways of avoiding the sacrifice of newborn babies; one was a magical procedure called molchomor, in which an animal—usually a lamb—was sacrificed in place of the child.

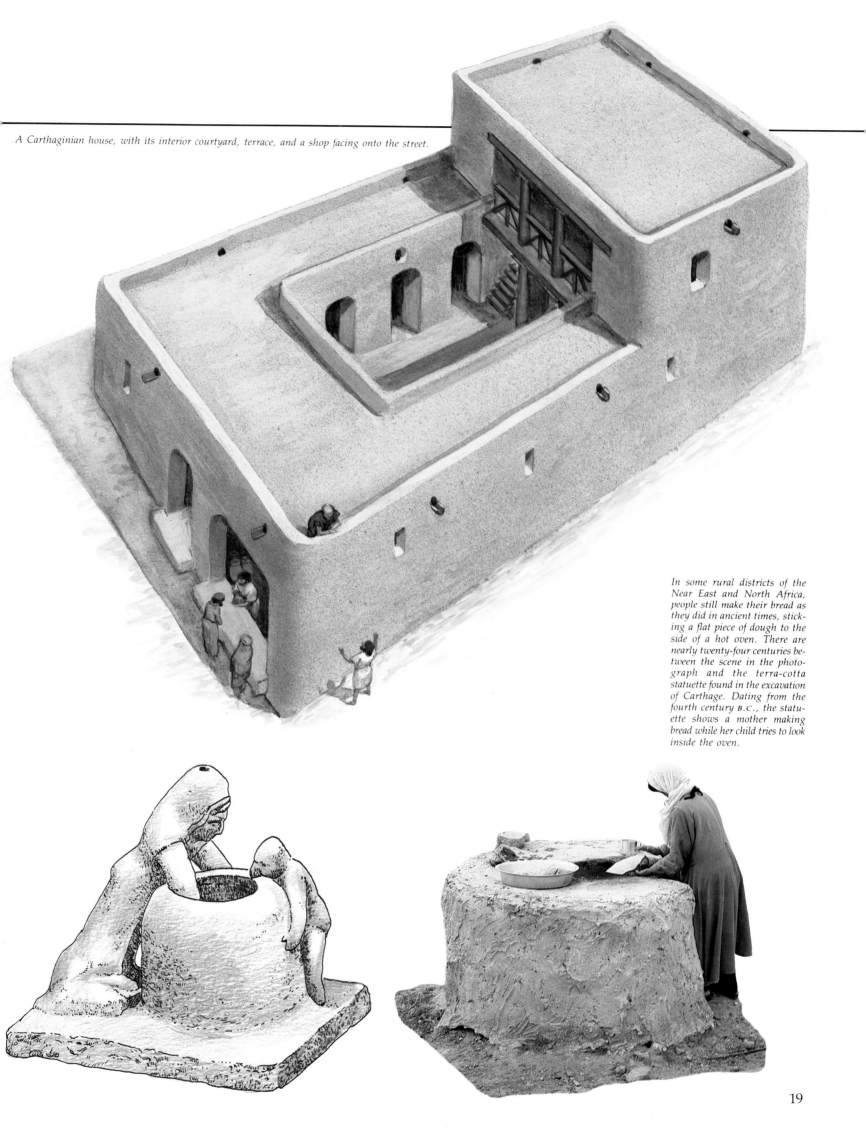

A Carthaginian house, with its interior courtyard, terrace, and a shop facing onto the street.

In some rural districts of the Near East and North Africa, people still make their bread as they did in ancient times, sticking a flat piece of dough to the side of a hot oven. There are nearly twenty-four centuries between the scene in the photograph and the terra-cotta statuette found in the excavation of Carthage. Dating from the fourth century B.C., the statuette shows a mother making bread while her child tries to look inside the oven.

19

THE ETRUSCANS

Long before Rome imposed its rule on Italy and the Mediterranean, the Etruscans, who came from Asia Minor, had established their high culture among the less developed Italic peoples. In a very real sense, they were civilizers, for it was they who built the first cities in Italy and thereby moved the Italians from the village to the urban mode of existence.

Within the boundaries of present-day Tuscany, the Etruscans founded several cities, ruled by kings; the most important among them joined forces in a powerful confederation. Thanks to the skills of their metallurgists, Etruscan warriors had powerful iron weapons. They conquered northern Italy as far as the Po River and seized Latium in the south, where they placed the Tarquin dynasty on the throne of the new city of Rome. Next they took control of the Campania and founded the town of Capua.

We know very little about the Etruscan way of life; we cannot read their texts, and the remains of their towns have all but disappeared. Only one town, Marzabotto (Misha in antiquity) in the south of Bologna, Italy, gives us an idea of how Etruscan towns were organized. Excavations have uncovered a network of roads laid out on a north-south and east-west grid. They were all constructed with drains and gutters. Rectangular blocks of buildings stood between the roads. Of the houses, only the outlines of the walls are left; most had courtyards containing wells. Various living rooms opened onto the courtyard. Numerous craftworkers, potters, and metal workers had their workshops along the main thoroughfare, where commercial activities must have been concentrated. The town had three temples, grouped together on a small hill; their timber and clay walls were built on stone foundations. Rome, which was ruled by Etruscan kings for a century, was built on this model.

Etruscan society was dominated by powerful aristocratic families. They were wealthy, owning huge farming estates, and they often led idle lives in which feasting and entertainment featured strongly. It was not unusual for a family to employ athletes, musicians, and artists to add to the pleasures of their leisure hours.

In the sixth century B.C., Etruscan power reached its height. But then it came up against Greek colonial expansion in the south of Italy. As a countermeasure the Etruscans entered into an alliance with the Carthaginians. Around 540 B.C. they took part in a ferocious naval battle, pitting their 120 vessels against 60 Greek galleys from the Phocaean colony in Corsica. Despite their numerical inferiority, the Greeks defeated the allies, though the Greeks then withdrew for fear of a renewed attack.

In 474 B.C. it was the Greeks' turn to take the initiative: their Syracusian fleet joined with the fleet of the Cumae and routed the Etruscan navy. Shortly afterwards the Samnites came down from the Apennine Mountains and drove the Etruscans out of the Campania. Finally, in the third century B.C., Rome wiped out all that remained of Etruscan power, seizing its cities one after the other.

The Etruscans were extraordinary metalworkers. They were famous in antiquity for their mastery of the manufacture of objects of iron, lead, tin, silver, and above all, bronze. Helped by the nearness of rich mines, which they exploited in a rational manner, the Etruscan metalworkers created a large quantity of mirrors, fine jewelry, large tripods, statuettes, ornaments, and formidable weapons.

If we can believe the many works of art, the Etruscans were fond of parties and banquets, where they reclined on couches, their elbows propped up on cushions. In contrast to what happened among the Greeks and the Romans, Etruscan women participated in many activities of public life, and their role in the family was often equal to that of the men.

The Etruscan bronzesmiths produced remarkable statues, vases, mirrors, and cistes, finely engraved metal boxes. The artisans were also past masters in appliqués of bronze, as is seen on this war chariot.

THE TOMBS OF THE DEAD

Most of our knowledge about the Etruscans comes not from the sparse remains of their cities and temples but from their *necropolises* ("cities of the dead"), which have been wonderfully well preserved.

At an Etruscan funeral the body would be laid out on a wagon, and the family and friends of the deceased would gather around. The ceremony was enlivened with music and dancing, as if it were an ordinary banquet. Then everyone present accompanied the dead person to his tomb, together with women mourners whose wailing alternated with funereal chanting.

The Etruscans had other, less pleasant funeral customs, which were reflected in the later Roman games. They organized armed combats between prisoners or handed captives over to wild animals. A painting on a tomb in Tarquinia depicts a man armed with a stick, a sack over his head, confronting a mastiff, which is being goaded forward by the master of the games. The object of these practices, reminiscent of human sacrifice, was to provide the deceased with the victims' blood as a guarantee of eternal life.

The tombs of the most privileged families were cut out of rock and were just like houses inside. Furniture, weapons, everyday objects, and clothes were laid out as offerings, either painted on the walls or carved. A great number of these tombs have several rooms; in each room, funeral beds are placed along the walls, with seats at their head.

The souls of the dead were carried away or accompanied by a winged spirit who led them to an eternal dwelling place, similar to the underworld of Greek mythology. This is illustrated in a large number of carvings, which show the dead person making his last journey on foot, on horseback, in a chariot, or sometimes in a boat.

In the Etruscan civilization, women enjoyed a freedom and independence that might well have been envied by the Greek women of their day and, later, by Roman women. Etruscan women had an important place in society; they could take part in ceremonies and attend public entertainments, the games in the arena, and boxing matches. They were allowed to take part in banquets, reclining on their elbows and sharing couches with men. This gave them a terrible reputation throughout the Mediterranean, where it was customary for the sexes to remain separate.

One proof of the importance of women in Etruscan society is provided by the funeral inscriptions that mention the names not only of the fathers of the dead but also of their mothers. Etruscan women could also play a part in politics. The Roman writer Livy stresses the role of Queen Tanaquil, who made her husband, Tarquinius Priscus, king of Rome. When he died, she ensured that her son-in-law, Servius Tullius, succeeded to the throne.

THE NECROPOLIS OF CERVETERI

The name Cerveteri comes from Caere Vetere, ("ancient Caere"), which belonged to the confederation of twelve Etruscan cities. The town was ruined and rebuilt many times, and nothing is left of it today. But the cemeteries built outside the town are almost completely intact. Caere was surrounded by three large groups of tombs, including the Banditaccia, one of the most extraordinary cemeteries of the ancient world. There are hundreds of tombs, buried under tumuli, and built like houses. They stand in rows along paths that cross the surface of the plateau or dip down into gulleys.

This Etruscan sarcophagus, found in a tomb at Cerveteri, dates from the sixth century B.C. and is typical of funeral art. The portrait of the husband and wife lying on a couch, tenderly united and eternally serene, is evidence that Etruscan customs were very different from those of most of the Greeks. The couch symbolizes the meal, which was eaten lying down. An enjoyable occasion in life, the dead would repeat it in the afterlife. Other Etruscan religious practices included looking into the future and reading omens. Priests, augurs, and haruspices (diviners) held the keys to the meaning of signs sent by the gods. Omens were seen in the entrails of sacrificed animals, the flight of birds, and lightning flashes, and they were interpreted according to strict rules. A bronze medal of an animal liver, carrying inscriptions and marked out in quarters, has even been found; its purpose was to be a guide for the haruspices in the art of divination.

An Etruscan tomb

Among the multitude of tombs at Cerveteri, the Tomb of the Reliefs (fourth century B.C.) is cut deep into the rock and is approached by a long staircase descending between two high walls. In the single room are inscriptions telling us that the tomb housed the remains of the Matuna family. Fourteen alcoves containing funeral couches are set into the walls. Holes for the bodies are set in benches, which take up most of the floorspace. Two thick pillars hold up the roof, which is made of two slightly sloping panels. On all the vertical surfaces, everyday objects, life-sized tools, weapons, and utensils are sculpted or applied in stucco.

GREEK CITIES

After the end of the Mycenaean civilization, the Greek world went through a Dark Age, which lasted for some centuries. During this Dark Age, villages lived self-enclosed lives, with few outside contacts; there were hardly any stone buildings. But iron metallurgy began to spread from the Near East, and as farming implements and weapons were forged, agriculture, hunting, and military defense developed and gained importance. Gradually the Greeks recovered a certain amount of prosperity and began to gather in cities around local kings, who were endowed with religious authority. Temples and sanctuaries were built on the acropolises, the "high cities," that dominated the towns. Goldsmiths, sculptors, and bronzesmiths developed both creativity and skill, producing original pieces that could be considered works of art. But several more centuries had to pass before Greek culture was to shine with its full brilliance, when the Archaic period of the seventh and sixth centuries B.C. was followed by the Classical period in the fifth and fourth centuries B.C.

Greek nationality was defined by belonging to a *polis*, or city-state. A *polis* included not just the city one lived in but also the surrounding countryside, villages, and hamlets. If you were to approach a Greek city between the sixth and second centuries B.C., the first thing to come into view would be its network of defenses, a fortress built on high and massive fortified walls. Very often fields and groves lay within the area between the ramparts and the town to protect the local people from starvation during a siege.

Every town had its main public square, the *agora*, where the citizens met and public buildings were concentrated; there one could find the council chamber, the tribunal, temples and shrines, shops and stalls. The other large buildings, devoted to education and health and leisure pursuits, were built elsewhere in the town or close by, depending on how much space they needed. The most important were the gymnasium, which was both a sports and an educational establishment; the sports stadium; the public baths; and the theater.

In ancient Greece the social and political structure often varied from town to town. In Sparta, for instance, society was based on a hierarchy: at the top were the Spartans, who held all the power; then came the *perioeci*, who had no rights but were free; and lastly the *helots*, serfs attached to the land, who could be mistreated and even killed with impunity.

The population of Athens was divided into citizens (150,000 in the fifth century B.C.); metics (35,000), foreigners who had settled there and had to pay taxes and do military service but were otherwise free; and slaves (80,000, men, women, and children), who only had one hope—to be freed one day by their masters.

From the fifth century B.C. onward, political power in many cities was in the hands of an assembly of male citizens. Administrative and judicial duties were allocated to their members, either by election or by a system of drawing lots. The leading role given to the *demos* ("the people") was at the roots of the concept of democracy.

One of man's most important inventions—money—occurred at the beginning of the seventh century B.C. The oldest known coins, made of gold, silver, or an alloy of the two, were minted at Aegina in Greece, and in Lydia, a kingdom in Asia Minor. During the sixth century B.C., the use of money spread throughout the whole Greek world. The units were distinguished by weight: the talenton *(equivalent to about 84 pounds) was divided into 60* minai, *a mina into 100* drachmai, *and a* drachma *into 6* oboloi. *Coins were made in bronze, silver, and gold; their appearance and the value of the metal varied greatly between different cities. Some cities, like Athens, used nothing but silver for a long time; others, like Sparta, took several centuries to start producing their own coinage.*

The *agora*: the focal point of Greek life, symbol of the city, and center of trade.

In the ancient markets the three basic Mediterranean products were sold—wheat, grapes, and olives. Olive oil had all kinds of daily uses, such as cooking, lighting, and cleaning; athletes covered their bodies in it, and elegant women used it in their cosmetics. It was also given in offering to the gods. But growing olives was a slow, difficult business. It takes ten to twelve years for trees to produce a crop, and the trees are susceptible to frost. Olive trees were of such all-around value that their destruction by an enemy was regarded as an unforgivable crime.

Greek society, like all ancient societies, was founded on slavery. Slaves were former prisoners of war, citizens who had lost their money, or the offspring of slaves. They could only attain the dignity of citizenship by saving their wages to buy their freedom, through the generosity of a rich benefactor, or by being granted freedom by their master. In Athens and all the other Greek cities, the condition of slaves depended very much on their owners and the kind of work and responsibilities the slaves were given. To be a preceptor, manager of a large estate, or a craftworker was far preferable to being a laborer in the Laurion mines.

FARM LABOR AND TOWN CRAFTS

Two writers several centuries apart, Hesiod, a poet, (eighth century B.C.) and Xenophon, a historian, (430 B.C.–354 B.C.), described country life in ancient Greece in very similar terms. Some of their descriptions could still apply to the lives of Mediterranean peasants today, as if farm labor has been untouched by time.

There were three types of farmers: the *autourgoi*, farmers who owned a little land and did the work themselves, assisted by family members or by a few slaves; farmers who owned somewhat more land and simply directed and supervised the work; and finally, the wealthy landowners who lived in towns and had managers to look after their estates.

The methods used to farm the wheatfields, olive groves, and vineyards were basic. The soil was roughly turned with a plow, drawn by mules in some areas and by oxen in others. Sickles were used to harvest the wheat. The grain was trampled by mules or oxen on a threshing floor and then, loaded in baskets, winnowed to separate the grain from the chaff. Finally the grain was ground into flour, either by mortar and pestle or in a stone mill worked by hand.

Around the houses were planted fruit trees, especially fig trees, and kitchen gardens where cabbages, garlic, lentils, and onions were grown. And every farmhouse had its beehives.

The Greeks herded a large number of sheep, goats, and pigs. Cattle and horses were rare, except in the rich pasturelands of Thessaly in the north; however, donkeys and mules were often used for carrying and pulling loads.

The Greek farmer had an advantage over the city dweller in that he could produce and even make almost everything he needed. He could feed his family and slaves, and make some of his own tools, while his wife spun wool from the sheep and wove it to make clothes. But, like the city dweller, he did have to buy larger and more complex equipment from expert craftworkers.

The artisans plied their trade mainly in the agora and the streets nearby. Some quarters were specialized, like the Keramaikos district, where most of the potters were to be found. The Greeks became expert potters, using skillful manufacturing techniques and producing their famous vases with a variety of shapes and decorative patterns. They had the potter's wheel, which enabled them to produce fine, evenly shaped vessels.

The second most important craft in the Greek world was metalworking, as can be seen on their vase paintings; some of these provide detailed pictures of work in forges, where the iron was hammered and cast, and bronze was beaten into shape. Leatherworkers gathered in the cities, too, along with tanners and shoemakers; carpenters and joiners; sculptors of wood, ivory, and stone; dyers; and of course armorers.

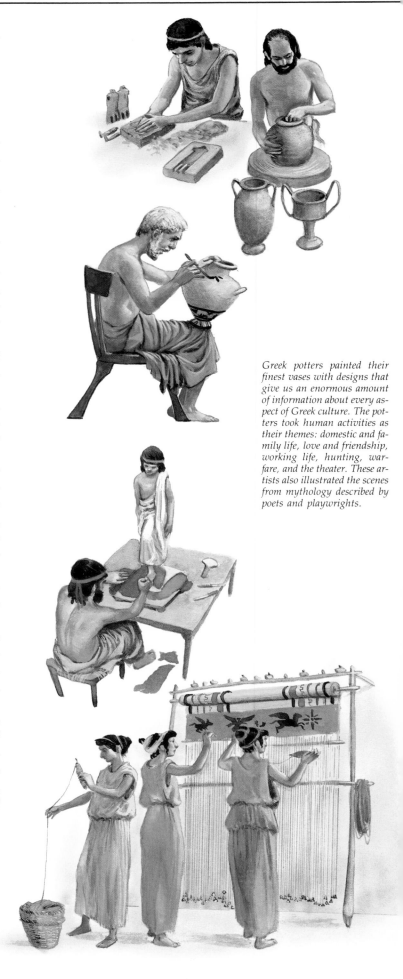

Greek potters painted their finest vases with designs that give us an enormous amount of information about every aspect of Greek culture. The potters took human activities as their themes: domestic and family life, love and friendship, working life, hunting, warfare, and the theater. These artists also illustrated the scenes from mythology described by poets and playwrights.

THE RULES OF CITY LIFE

Magistrates called astynomoi were given the task of seeing that Greek cities were kept clean and orderly. There was a long list of regulations for

• safety during festivals
• the control of dancers, musicians, and courtesans
• keeping the streets in good repair
• the collection of garbage and its disposal at the public dump
• the maintenance of waterpipes, fountains, and reservoirs
• ensuring that fountains were not used for washing objects or clothes or by animals (who had to drink at special basins downstream of the fountains)

• the maintenance of public lavatories and sewers
• keeping public thoroughfares clear of building rubble, holes, and open drains
• preventing building in public spaces
• making sure the streets were perfectly clean before processions
• cleaning altars and statues before religious festivals
• imposing fines on people who violated the regulations, and for seeing that the fines were collected

Control of the commercial police and the markets was put in the hands of other municipal officers, called agoranomoi.

ATHENS IN THE FIFTH CENTURY B.C.

According to legend it was Theseus, slayer of the Minotaur, who united the twelve villages of Attica in a single city—Athens. The historical facts are simpler. The city gradually grew up around its acropolis, thanks to a wealth of local natural resources. It benefited from a plain rich in wheat, hillsides where vines and olive trees grew, and the Aegean Sea close by, which favored both fishing and trade. As soon as money replaced barter, Athens was also able to profit from the rich silver mines of Laurion nearby. The great marble quarries of Mount Pendelikon, also close by, supplied the Athenians with the material for the superb buildings that declared the glory of Athens in the fifth century B.C.

By then the city and its suburbs had tens of thousands of inhabitants, citizens, metics, and slaves. After the reforms of the poet turned statesman Solon (about 640 B.C.–560 B.C.), every Athenian citizen over twenty could take part in the government of the state by attending the people's assembly, the *ecclesia*, which met at least four times a month. Many citizens could not attend the assembly because they were busy in their fields or workshops. But the presence of six thousand members was enough to carry through decisions affecting the rights of all the citizens.

The permanent assembly of Athens was the *Boule*, or Senate. It was composed of five hundred members over the age of thirty, drawn from among the citizens by lot. The *Boule* ensured that the laws promulgated by the *ecclesia* were carried out, supervised the magistrates, and received ambassadors. Every day an *epistates*, a chief of state, was chosen by lot; he kept the seal of Athens and the keys of the temples in which the public treasury was kept. Athens was thus the only regime in the world where, without a doubt, any citizen might hope one day to be president! In fact, the real power belonged to ten *archons* in charge of religious festivals, and to ten *strategoi*, generals who commanded the armed fleet, negotiated treaties, and convened the *ecclesia*. Pericles, the most famous Athenian statesman of the fifth century B.C., was reelected as a *strategus* for fourteen years in succession, from 443 B.C. until his death in 429.

Justice was the province of *heliasts*, judges drawn by lot, who had to decide on cases within a single day. Immediately after the speeches had finished, the judges cast their votes. If the accused was judged guilty by a small margin of votes, he could choose an alternate punishment to that imposed by the judges. It was usually accepted by the court. Socrates, the great philosopher accused of corrupting youth with his teachings and life-style, showed his lack of respect for the judges by choosing an impossible punishment. He paid for this by being instantly condemned to commit suicide by drinking hemlock.

The great pride of Athens in the fifth century B.C. was its defeat of the Persians, first on land at Marathon in 490 B.C. and then at sea at Salamis ten years later. Emboldened by its prestige, Athens placed itself at the head of a number of cities in the Confederacy of Delos, while its rival Sparta formed the Peloponnesian League. The war between the two cities, punctuated by truces, ended with the defeat of Athens in 404 B.C.

The Panathenaic Festival was held once a year in honor of the goddess Athena, protectress of the city. Every four years a larger version was held, in which an ancient wooden statue of the goddess, kept in a temple called the Erechtheum, was dressed in a beautifully embroidered robe, the sacred peplos. *This had been woven during the previous nine months by girls seven to twelve years old who lived in the House of the Arrhephoria. The whole city took part in the Greater Panathenaea. The magistrates and priests led the procession; then came the old men and women holding olive branches. The metics carried small boats as tokens of their foreign origins. At the end of the column came the Athenian cavalry dressed in traveling costume.*

In the fifth century the Acropolis of Athens consisted of a collection of monumental buildings, among the most magnificent in the Greek world. At the center of the sacred hill stood the Parthenon, the great temple of Athena, built between 447 B.C. and 432 B.C. To its left was the Erechtheum, built between 421 B.C. and 405 B.C., which housed several ancient shrines and sacred objects. It was decorated with Caryatides, and in its western courtyard stood a sacred olive tree. (Athena had caused it to grow there during a quarrel with Poseidon, to establish her rights over Attica.) The Acropolis was entered via the Propylaea, the five-doored entrance built of marble between 437 B.C. and 431 B.C. Its north wing, the Pinacotheca was a picture gallery. At the south end was the temple of Athena Nike ("Athena Victorious"). The most remarkable monument on the Acropolis was a colossal statue of Athena, nearly 30 feet high, which watched over all of Attica. From the port of Piraeus, the sailors could see the tip of Athena's spear glinting in the rays of the sun.

WARFARE

The Greeks enjoyed war more than most people of antiquity. From the seventh to the second century B.C., they rarely stopped fighting, either against each other or united against the threat of the Persian army.

Boys were given a highly structured military training. In Athens, from about the age of twelve, young citizens began physical training under the direction of *paidotribes*, to develop their bodies and begin learning military skills. The schools were divided into two classes—one for boys of twelve to fifteen and one for youths of fifteen to eighteen. Here they trained in the *palaestra* in gymnastics, long jump, wrestling, and throwing the discus and javelin. They went to the stadium to take part in races; later, as experienced athletes, they would return there to compete for the glory of their city.

Athenians could be called on to serve their country when needed at any age from eighteen to sixty. Between the ages of eighteen and twenty, young men learned to handle weapons and took part in military maneuvers. Having already developed skill in throwing the javelin, they were now taught the use of the shield, lance, and sword; how to wear a helmet, breastplate, and leg armor; and how to use a bow. Bows had fallen into disuse after the Homeric period, but they reappeared as weapons in the Athenian army at the beginning of the fifth century B.C. as a result of Persian influence.

After two years of training, and service in a fortress at Piraeus or on the frontier, the *ephebus*, or young soldier, was then ready to serve as a *hoplite*. Hoplites were frontline troops, who carried the *hoplon*, or shield; they continued as such until the age of fifty. After that, they could be mobilized to guard the city in a territorial unit.

In Sparta, where military prowess was of utmost importance, *hoplites* were given a far stricter program of training than in other parts of Greece. At the age of seven, young Spartans were separated from their mothers and entered into the state educational system, which was entirely oriented toward military training. Their education continued until they reached the age of sixteen. The Greek historian Plutarch tells us that as far as culture was concerned, this education was ''limited to basic requirements, all the rest consisting of learning to obey orders, withstand fatigue, and win in battle. This is why their training becomes increasingly hard as they grow older.''

From the age of twelve, their only garment was a cloak, all year long; discipline became stricter, and any mistake, however slight, was punished with the whip. They were given insufficient food so that they might learn to obtain their own by hunting or stealing. They always ate communally; on feast days they were given a single dish, black broth, consisting of pork meat and blood mixed in vinegar and highly spiced and salted. The rest of the time they had to be content with barley cakes garnished with olives and onions.

Poor citizens, metics, and slaves often accompanied the armies on campaigns. They carried the hoplites' arms and baggage, and took part in the fighting, armed with bows, javelins, and slings with which they could throw clay, lead, or bronze missiles with deadly force.

A Greek army consisted basically of foot soldiers. There was a small cavalry reserved for the wealthiest citizens, the only ones who could afford to buy and keep horses. Horsemen rode bareback, with no saddle or stirrups; they fought with a sword or two spears carried onto the battlefield by their orderlies. The core of the army was the hoplites, foot soldiers equipped with the hoplon, a large round shield carried on the left arm. Hoplites also wore crested helmets, which covered their head, neck, nose, and cheeks. Protection for the chest and abdomen was provided by cuirasses made of metal or layers of linen. The legs were protected by armor called greaves. Weapons consisted of a wooden spear with a metal tip, a double-edged sword, and a dagger. Hoplites from all the different Greek peoples were equipped in the same fash-

ion except for the Spartans, who wore tunics dyed red to disguise bloodstains.

In the fourth century B.C., the Macedonians perfected their formidable phalanxes. The phalanxes were composed of several lines of hoplites armed with long spears, presenting the enemy with a solid wall of spears that was almost impossible to attack head on. In Athens, military power was also measured by the war fleet, consisting of dozens of triremes, or galleys with three rows of oarsmen. Swift to maneuver, these ships were extremely efficient and gave Athens control of the Aegean Sea from the port of Piraeus. Piraeus was linked to the city by long walls, massive ramparts protecting the route between Athens and her gateway to the sea.

GREEK COLONIES

The Greek word for colony was *apoikia*, which contains the idea of a home away from home. The first colonies were created in Asia Minor, with the migrations of the Mycenaeans. Later on, in the period between 750 B.C. and 550 B.C., the cities of the Greek world sent out bands of their citizens to settle Gaul, Sicily, Spain, southern Italy, the area that is now Libya, and the shores of the Black Sea. These colonies were completely independent of their mother cities, whose only hold on them were cultural memories and economic relations. This two-century expansion of the Greek world can be attributed to overpopulation, social unrest, and economic advantage.

Later on, after Alexander the Great's conquests in the fourth century B.C., the Greeks founded new colonies in the East. Their culture had a profound influence on Egypt, Syria, Persia, and lands as far as the Indian border of Afghanistan. At the end of the fourth century B.C., Hellenism, as the Greek culture of this period is known, had reached its maximum expansion. From Spain to the Indus River, Greek travelers were welcomed in colonies and trading stations occupied by fellow Greeks who shared their language, beliefs, and customs.

Among the most famous colonies were Massilia (Marseilles), founded by Greeks from Phocaea in Asia Minor; Syracuse, founded by emigrants from Corinth; and Sybaris, founded by Achaean Greeks. These colonies were loyal to Athens, but they enjoyed complete independence and created other colonies in their turn; the Syracusians founded Camarina and Akrai, and the Sybarites founded Metapontum and Paestum.

These autonomous colonies were usually rich and powerful; there were also other settlements, *klerouchiai*, which remained entirely allied and subordinate to the city-state. In the Athenian klerouchia, first founded on the isle of Euboea and then in the various Aegean Islands, Athens allocated plots of land to its poorest citizens by a system of *kleros*, or drawing lots.

Before people decided to emigrate, the oracle had to be consulted and the god's prophetic advice heard through the mouth of a priest or priestess. The most famous oracles were dedicated to Apollo, at Delphi, and to Zeus, at Dodona. The city would send a delegation to question the god about the timing of the departure, the choice of country, and the exact location of the town to be built there. Once the decision was made, the metropolis assembled all those who wanted to take part in the venture. Most were poor citizens, people who had lost their money, or metics. In the new city everyone would be equal. Some authoritarian regimes took advantage of the opportunity to put political opponents on the list of emigrants. Sometimes, to ease the strain on a city, lots would be drawn to send one male child per family. Led by an oikistes the travelers left with their baggage, their animals, and sacred fire taken from the altar of Hestia, guardian goddess of the city and the family; this sacred fire would be used to light the first fire in the new settlement. When the colonists disembarked, they would offer sacrifices to the gods. Then the surveyors and architects would start planning and building the new town.

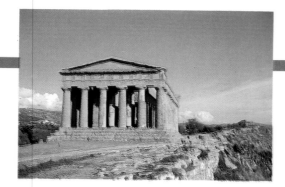

MAGNA GRAECIA

Sicily and southern Italy were colonized by the Greeks to such an extent that the region came to be called Magna Graecia ("Great Greece"). At Segesta, Selinonte, Syracuse, and Paestum, great cities grew up, and their power was affirmed by superb buildings—temples, theaters, and city walls. At Agrigen- *to six temples were built, including the Temple of Concord, with an elegant facade ornamented by six Doric columns. Gems of Greek architecture are often found in Sicily, southern Italy, and Asia Minor rather than in Greece itself.*

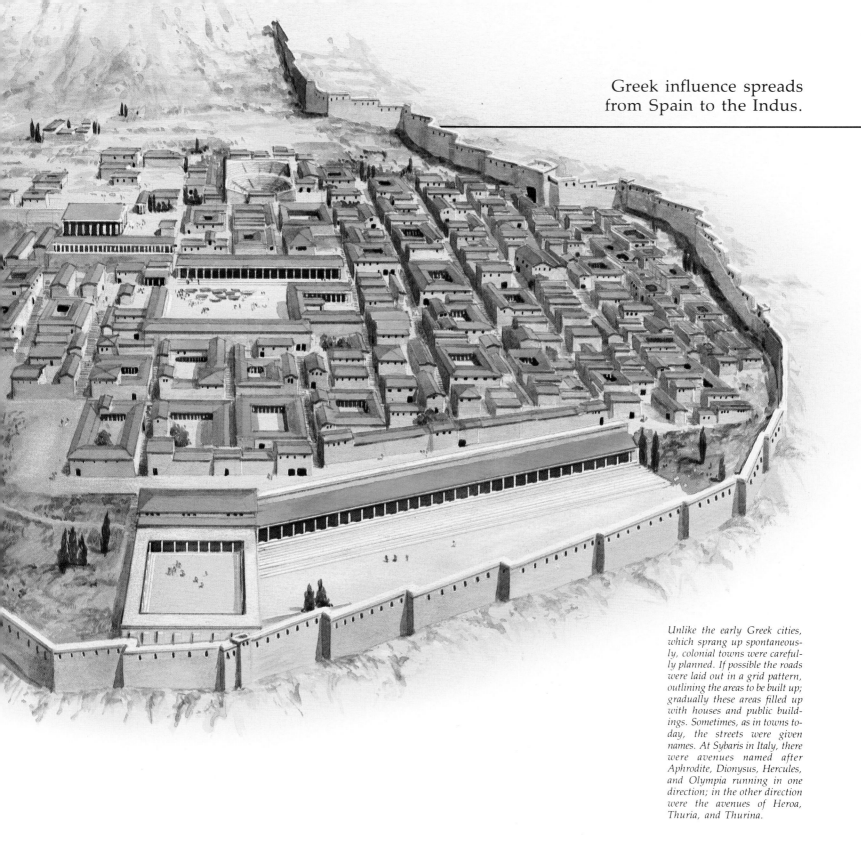

Unlike the early Greek cities, which sprang up spontaneously, colonial towns were carefully planned. If possible the roads were laid out in a grid pattern, outlining the areas to be built up; gradually these areas filled up with houses and public buildings. Sometimes, as in towns today, the streets were given names. At Sybaris in Italy, there were avenues named after Aphrodite, Dionysus, Hercules, and Olympia running in one direction; in the other direction were the avenues of Heroa, Thuria, and Thurina.

This coin from Massilia (Marseilles) is an example of the wealth of many Greek colonies. The legend of the founding of Marseilles recounts that two Greek sailors landed on the coast the very day the local king was marrying off his daughter; she had the right to choose her husband freely from among those present. Her choice fell on one of the sailors, which led to the foundation of the town. Marseilles's trade was based on Mediterranean agricultural produce, tin, amber from the Baltic, and silver, from which coins could be made.

The emigrants left to found their new colonies sailing in merchant vessels, similar to those that sailed up and down the coasts. The vessels were around 50 feet long, equipped with square sails and with steering oars; these vessels were easy to maneuver and could sail against the wind. All kinds of timber went into their construction. The keel was of cypress wood, the masts of cedar, the tenon and mortise joints of oak, the planks of pine, and the laths of the hull of elm.

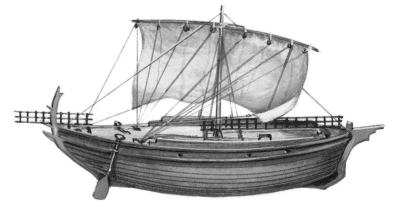

THE GODS AND THEIR TEMPLES

In Neolithic Greece and in the Cretan civilization, religious belief focused mainly on the cult of mother goddesses who looked after the fertility of animals and the soil. In the second millennium B.C., Indo-European invaders called Achaeans brought with them a new pantheon of largely male deities. By the Mycenaean period, the religion practiced was a synthesis of local and Achaean beliefs.

Around 1100 B.C. the invasion of the Dorians, with their warlike traditions, introduced a patriarchal approach to culture and religion. Zeus, lord of heaven, took his place as chief god, Poseidon ruled the ocean, and Hades reigned in the underworld, while around them revolved a multitude of gods and goddesses with varying powers and functions.

Around 800 B.C., when the Greek cities were being founded, it became the custom to create shrines for the worship of local protecting deities. The ordinary people were more drawn to Dionysus, the god of wine, and fertility; the goddesses Demeter and Kore, who looked after the crops and harvests; and Aesculapius, who cured the sick. The worship of these deities gave rise to initiation rites and "mysteries" offering worshipers the hope of eternal life.

In the fifth century B.C., Greeks everywhere shared the same gods and the same rituals. People thronged to the great Panhellenic shrines at Athens, Olympia, Delphi, Delos, and Dodona, ladened with gifts and offerings.

With very rare exception (such as Pan with his goat's hooves), the Greek gods were depicted as human beings and as a rule, they behaved like flesh-and-blood people. The myths recount, in a tolerant fashion, the numerous vagaries of their lives, their loves, their hates, and their rivalries—in which human beings were generally the losers.

In the eighth and seventh centuries B.C., Delphi became one of the great sanctuaries of the Greek world. Every city had a treasury built there to house offerings. In 490 B.C., the Athenian treasury was dedicated with part of the booty captured from the Persians after the Battle of Marathon. The Athenian treasury was a rectangular marble building in the Doric style, ornamented with sculptures of the adventures of Hercules and Theseus.

Human beings had to beware of the wrath of Zeus, lord of thunder; of Poseidon, who commanded tempests and unleashed earthquakes; and of Hades, who awaited them on "the other side." Apollo, son of Zeus, and god of beauty and prophecy, was closer to mortals and kinder to them; he was happy to advise them through the Pythian oracle at Delphi. Surprisingly, Ares, god of war, was not highly revered by the Greeks; they preferred Athena, goddess of wisdom and the arts, who was born from Zeus' head; Aphrodite, goddess of love; and Dionysus, god of wine and pleasure.

The gods and goddesses lived on Mount Olympus. There, hidden from mortal eyes by a veil of clouds, they feasted on ambrosia and nectar while they listened to the songs of the Muses.

Zeus

Hera, sister and wife of Zeus

Hermes, messenger of the gods

Hephaestus, son of Zeus and Hera and god of fire

Athena, goddess of war, wisdom, and the arts

Aphrodite, goddess of love and beauty

All religious ceremonies were accompanied by animal sacrifices and offerings of food. Valuable objects, statues, precious dishes, and war trophies would be placed around the sanctuaries or in the treasuries designed for this purpose. The first sacred centers were natural sites—springs, grottos, woods and ravines—inhabited or visited by the god. In the sixth century B.C., temples began to be built at these shrines to house the gods. The temples were stone buildings with colonnades, often impressive in size. In the following century, Greek temples reached a stage of perfection, both in their proportions and in the quality of the stonework, sculpture, and decorations. In the huge main hall of these majestic buildings, where the ancestral fire burned, stood the statue of the god or goddess, often taking up the full height of the building. The colossal chryselephantine statue of Zeus at Olympia became one of the wonders of the world. The god's clothing was of solid gold (chrysos) and his flesh made of ivory (elephantos).

When someone died, a coin was slipped between the person's teeth so that he or she could pay Charon, the boatman of the underworld. Then the body was washed, perfumed, and wrapped in three white sheets. It was buried the next day before sunrise.

Tombs stood along the sides of the roads leading out of towns. At Athens the main cemetery was in the Kerameikos quarter. The corpse was placed directly into the grave or enclosed in a coffin. The grave was then covered with a mound of earth, on top of which was placed a marble stela, often in the shape of a lecythus, a large urn symbolizing the funeral rites.

Poseidon,
brother of Zeus
and god of the sea

Artemis,
Apollo's twin sister
and goddess of hunting

Hestia,
goddess of the hearth

Demeter,
goddess of the harvest

Ares,
son of Zeus and Hera
and god of war

Apollo,
god of beauty, music, and prophecy

35

PHILOSOPHERS AND ACTORS

In ancient Greece, philosophers and actors, each in their own way, employed dialogue, speeches, and words to describe and account for the reality of the world and human behavior. Upon occasion, they even used similar talents. The eloquence of Socrates, for example, so charmed the Athenians that at some of their banquets, they entertained themselves with philosophical discourses on love and death rather than with drinking songs!

The first *philosophoi* ("lovers of wisdom") were scholars seeking a logical explanation for natural phenomena and for the world and its origins. In the sixth century B.C., Thales of Miletus was the first to try to find the principle of the universe; he held that all things originated from water. One day as he walked and absent-mindedly gazed at the stars, he fell down a well, which made him look ridiculous in the eyes of his colleagues. However, he remained famous for correctly predicting the eclipse of the sun in 585 B.C.

During the same period, Pythagoras was trying to demonstrate that the universe was ordered according to mathematical laws. Starting from this principle, he worked out the famous geometrical theorem that is named after him. He studied the relationships between numbers and living beings, and made discoveries about the intervals between musical notes. He taught his followers that harmony was the principle of the universe, and he passed on his doctrine of the transmigration of souls.

For the first time, people were trying to find a rational, mechanistic explanation of the universe, with no recourse to mythology. Philosophy developed increasingly along these lines, though not without opposition. Anaxagoras, in the fifth century B.C., was exiled from Athens for asserting that the sun and the moon were not gods. And Socrates was condemned to die by drinking hemlock for, among other charges, the crime of not believing in the city gods, a charge that he denied. His philosophical thought was centered on problems concerning mankind and morality, and he passed on his ideas to followers like Plato, who in turn taught Aristotle.

During the Dionysian festivals in honor of the god of the vine and fertility, the Greek cities organized great drama and poetry competitions. At Athens, the whole city was expected to attend, and the state even donated two obols (coins) to the poor so that they could go. The fifteen thousand seats in the theaters at Athens and Epidaurus would be packed all day long. The spectacle began soon after sunrise and continued until the evening; four or five plays were performed throughout the day. The public bought food and drink there, and took an active part in the show, being generous with both applause and catcalls.

When these festivities were initiated in the sixth century B.C., the show simply consisted of a chorus singing the legend of Dionysus or some other mythological hero of ancient days. Then in the fifth century, a solo performer appeared, the protagonist, or starring actor, playing the part of the hero of the story. Soon the protagonist was joined by a second and then a third player. Drama had been born.

Philosophers had schools and disciples; they taught in the gymnasium, originally devoted to physical training. There the master would walk about, talking with his disciples. Today the word gymnasium is used in several languages to describe a school of secondary education. The French word lycée comes from the name of an Athenian gymnasion where Aristotle taught. The word academy, now meaning "a seat of learning," comes from the name of the park just outside Athens called Academus where Plato set up his school of philosophy.

The Greek thinkers explain the world in physical terms and expound on human passions.

The Greek theatron was a semicircular theater with seats built up on a hillside. At the foot was a circular area, the orchestra, where the chorus sang and danced. Behind this was a wall, the skene, on which scenes were painted on movable panels. In front of it the principal actors played on a raised stage, the proskenion. Their action was accompanied by a commentary from the chorus, composed of twelve to fifteen choristers in a tragedy and twenty-four in a comedy. The actors moved from the orchestra to the proskenion according to the action of the play.

Greek actors were always men, even in women's roles. They all wore masks with exaggerated features, indicating to the audience whether the character was dramatic or comic. The masks had funnel-shaped mouths that amplified the voice. But, in fact, the accoustics in Greek theaters were so good that the actors' words could be heard clearly from the top seats. Plays were always in verse, with some parts declaimed, some sung, and some mimed. The author was also producer, director, and leader of the chorus. The great writers of tragedy of ancient Greece were Aeschylus, Sophocles, and Euripides; they based their works on contemporary events and traditional myths and legends. The authors of comedies, such as Aristophanes, satirized political personalities; the authors used caricature as a powerful form of criticism and protest.

THE OLYMPIC GAMES

The Olympic Games, in which athletes from all over the world take part, is the continuation of a purely Greek tradition. The modern games were founded in Athens in 1894 by a Frenchman, Pierre de Coubertin. He was recreating, after a gap of 1,502 years, the sporting event held at Olympia every four years, between 776 B.C. and 392 B.C.

Men from every Greek city competed in these Panhellenic games, but barbarians were excluded and so were women, who were not even allowed to watch; only Demeter's priestess was invited to Olympia. During the competitions, fighting between states and within cities was forbidden; a truce was called in political and public life, and it would have been sacrilege to start a war while the games were on.

Olympia lies in a hilly region, about 15 miles from the west coast of the Peloponnese in the province of Elis. This secluded, peaceful spot became the meeting place for Greeks from every point of the compass, and its name became famous throughout the ancient world. The history of Olympia from its inception has been recovered through excavations, which began in 1875.

At the start of the ninth century B.C., the inhabitants of a small village at the foot of the Hill of Kronus worshiped Zeus in a neighboring grove, the Altis, which was consecrated to him. The fact that the lord of Mount Olympus had a natural abode in this place (hence the name Olympia), explains why Zeus had no temple built for him at Olympia until the fifth century B.C.

The local people organized sporting competitions in honor of the chief god, and these rapidly became famous throughout Greece, although it is not known exactly why. The Olympian Games became so important that the Greeks later decided to organize their calendar in relation to the date when the games were first held, 776 B.C. Thus the date of the battle of Marathon, which for us is 490 B.C., was referred to by the Greeks as the second year of the seventy-second Olympiad.

The runners' starting line was marked by stone slabs with triangular grooves to provide a toe grip. Posts were fixed into square sockets to mark out each runner's place.

THE OLYMPIC STADIUM

The Olympian racetrack was surrounded by a simple grassy mound on which some twenty thousand people could gather. With the enormous number of competitors and spectators from all over the Hellenic world, the Olympian Games needed a lot of preparation. Two months before the starting date, officials called hellanodikoi received the competitors, taught them the rules, and held probationary trials to classify them by age and strength.

Races and combats in honor of Zeus.

The Olympian Games lasted seven days. They began with sacrifices to Zeus; then the athletes made a solemn oath to abide by the rules. For the next five days, the competitions were held; all the competitors took part naked in an order decided by lot. In the fifth century B.C., the contests began with footraces run over various distances and relay races. The marathon, which today commemorates the achievements of a Greek warrior, did not exist in antiquity. The toughest contest was a race in which the runners wore the heavy armor of a hoplite. Then came the most prized contest, the pentathlon, which combined the five skills of running, throwing the discus, throwing the javelin, wrestling, and the long jump. Other single contests followed: wrestling, boxing (with the hands bound in leather thongs), and pancratium, an extremely violent form of combat in which any kind of blow, hold, or twist was allowed except for gouging out one's opponent's eyes! Bouts only came to an end when one of the participants passed out or even died—or, less drastically, lifted his arm to signal defeat. The sixth day was devoted to horse-and-chariot racing. During these contests the riders, chariots, and spectators gathered in a larger arena, the hippodrome. Finally, the seventh and last day was spent celebrating the victory of the winners. The officials and athletes were conducted in a large procession to a banquet. At the end of the feast, a herald proclaimed the winners' names and the names of their fathers and home towns. The prizes were simple olive wreaths, but when the winners returned home victorious, the athletes were given a triumphal welcome and were often immortalized in poems and statues.

ALEXANDER THE GREAT

In the fourth century B.C., when the Greek city-states were being weakened by constant warfare among themselves, King Philip II of Macedonia gained control of the whole Greek peninsula. In 337 B.C. he set up the Corinthian League which, under his leadership, was dedicated to the freeing of the Greek cities of Asia Minor from Persian domination.

But Philip was assassinated the following year, and it was left to his son, Alexander III, to undertake the campaign. Alexander was twenty when he ascended the throne of Macedonia, but he already had had experience in ruling and leading troops. And he had been superbly educated.

In 334 B.C. he landed in Asia Minor with an army of thirty-one thousand foot soldiers and five thousand horsemen. Within a few years he conquered Asia Minor, Syria, Phoenicia, and Egypt, where he founded the city of Alexandria. Then he turned to Mesopotamia, where he decisively defeated Darius III.

But the vast territory he had conquered was not enough for Alexander. In 326 B.C. he crossed the Indus River, crushed the troops of the Indian rajah Porus, and decided to advance to the mouth of the Ganges River. But his troops were exhausted and refused to go on. Alexander was forced to turn back.

During the years of fighting and conquering, Alexander conceived an idea even more ambitious and grandiose than the subjugation of a vast empire. He intended to unite the world in a new order of peace, justice, and prosperity and in so doing, to create a new civilization, a combination of Greek and oriental elements. To rule this whole inhabitable world, the *oikumene*, a dynasty of mixed origin was needed; therefore he married three Persian princesses to make sure that this unity would exist at the highest level of society. Alexander also planned a great campaign aimed at conquering the Mediterranean Basin. But fate intervened to thwart his plans; he died of malaria in the summer of 323 B.C. at the age of 33.

THE BATTLE OF ISSUS

At the end of autumn in 333 B.C., Alexander had to confront the Persian army once again. Since Alexander's landing in Asia Minor, Darius of Persia had been steadily pushed back and was trying to bar Alexander's way into Syria. The battle took place at the town of Issus, near the coast. Despite a clever move by Darius, who managed to get behind the Greek army, Alexander's military genius won the day. Alexander approached Darius, who was forced to take flight in his chariot. When the Persians saw their king leave the field, they gave up the battle, leaving Darius's wife and family in Alexander's hands.

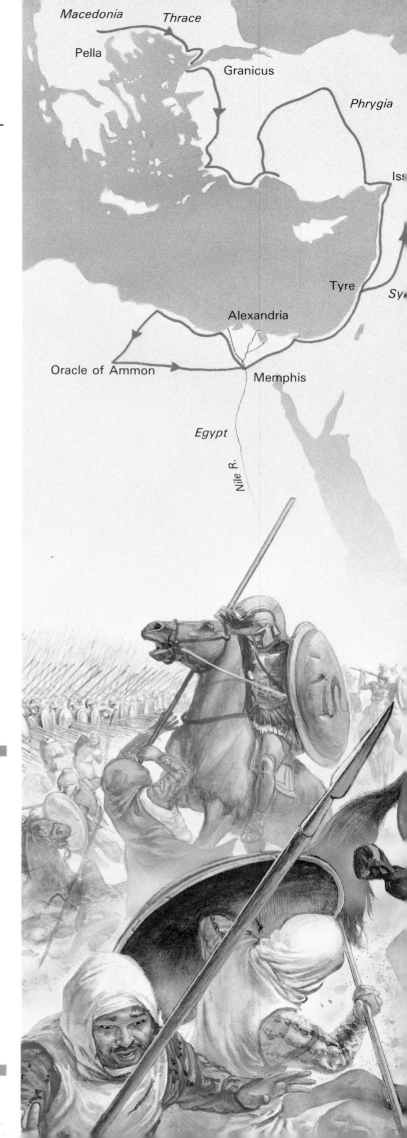

Armenia

Oxus R. (Amu-Darya)

Maracanda
(Samarkand)

Bactria
Badakshan

Gaugamela

Tigris R.

Ecbatana

Media

Parthia

Alexandria
(Herat)

Euphrates R.

Babylon

Susa

Alexandria
Arachosiae
(Kandahar)

Alexandria

Persis

Indus R.

Persepolis

Pattala

Hormuz

HELLENISTIC CIVILIZATION

W hen Alexander's generals conferred after their king's death, they decided to accept his infant son by Queen Roxana as their king, Alexander IV. Until he came of age, the empire was to be ruled by his generals, each of whom controlled a large portion of the great empire. These governors, who are known as Alexander's successors, the *diadochoi*, soon realized that even a part of so great an empire could be a mighty kingdom in itself. Consequently they began fighting among themselves. In 310 B.C. the path was cleared for the breakup of Alexander's empire by the murders of the remaining members of the royal family.

Until 281 B.C. the *diadochoi* were constantly at war. They employed mercenary armies of Macedonians and Greeks, and used increasingly large and powerful siege engines. Although wars were continuous for the half century after Alexander's death, they were comparatively humane, for the *diadochoi* were interested in maintaining the prosperity of the territories they occupied and the soldiers were professionals who were free from national hatreds.

At the end of these wars, the Hellenistic world settled down. There were three great kingdoms: Macedonia, ruled by the Antigonid dynasty; Syria, under the Seleucid dynasty; and Egypt, under the Ptolemaic dynasty. Other political units were the republic of Rhodes, in the Aegean Sea; the kingdom of Pergamum, in Asia Minor; and two federal states in Greece—the Achaean League and the Aetolian League. Once powerful Athens remained glorious only as a cultural and educational center, and mighty Sparta deteriorated to become a Williamsburg (Virginia), where tourists go to see how people lived in the old days.

From the time of Alexander's conquests and the wars of the *diadochoi*, the Greeks and their culture had been moving eastward. Alexander founded Greek cities, most of them called Alexandria, and his successors kept up the policy of bringing in Greek settlers. Naturally, Greek civilization had a great influence on the orientals, and the Greeks were changed by their association with the orientals. As a result a new civilization sprang up: the Hellenistic, or Greeklike civilization. It was very productive in the fields of philosophy, science, technology, literature, art, and religion. And when we compare it to the Hellenic civilization of pre-Alexander Greece, we find that it was much more tolerant of ethnic differences, much more cosmopolitan, and much more individualistic. At the height of the Hellenistic period, it was enough to dress like a Greek and speak Greek well to be considered a Greek. It was this civilization that was adopted by the Romans and passed on by them to the peoples of the western Mediterranean.

Having eliminated their great rival, the Carthaginians, at the end of the third century B.C., the Romans began a slow but inexorable expansion into the Greek world. With the defeat of Antiochus the Great of Syria in 188 B.C., Rome was the dominant power in the eastern Mediterranean. After the battle of Pydna in 168 B.C., all of Greece was subject to Rome. In 64 B.C., Pompey the Great conquered Asia Minor and Syria, and in 30 B.C. it was Egypt's turn to become a Roman province. Cleopatra VII, the last of the Hellenistic rulers, committed suicide.

Archimedes, born in Syracuse in 287 B.C., was the most famous scholar of antiquity. He placed his abilities and knowledge in the service of his native city, improved the design of the catapults positioned on the ramparts, and invented burning glasses to set fire to the Roman fleet. At the end of the siege of 212 B.C., while he was absorbed in drawing a geometric figure in the sand, he was killed by a Roman soldier—against the orders of the Roman authorities, who had wanted to employ him in the war against Carthage.

Archimedes' work covered an incredibly wide range, including physics, chemistry, geometry, mathematics, and astronomy. He was the first man to determine the exact value of π (pi) and the way to determine the specific gravity of solids.

*While science and technology were advancing at a pace that was never to be achieved under
the Romans, Hellenistic art, far from declining, was also astonishingly rich. Architects and
sculptors, in constant pursuit of perfection, decorated towns and sanctuaries with works of
unparalleled quality. In Asia Minor especially, where the cities benefited from oriental influences, Hellenistic art enjoyed its finest flowering. This can be seen even today in the remains of the Hellenistic towns on the Turkish coast. Contacts with this brilliant world aroused
in the Romans a desire for conquest; they wanted to model themselves on the Greeks and to
fill their public baths and palaces with marble and bronze statues, like this fighter at rest.*

With the spread of learning and new discoveries during the Hellenistic period,
scholars began to engage in new, deeper
forms of research. The Greek scholars who
lived in Alexandria in Egypt, the most fertile intellectual center of the Mediterranean, produced a quantity of inventions.
Ctesibius, an Alexandrian philosopher of
the second century B.C., was the first person to think of using compressed air as a
source of energy and of exploring the uses
of waterpower. He invented several clocks;
they told the time by means of a small figure holding a rod, which was slowly
pushed up a marked column by water pressure. Hero of Alexandria studied Ctesibius's inventions and writings and
improved on his techniques to harness the
power of steam. His "steam turbine," the
aeolipile, consisted of a sphere with two
escape nozzles, powered by steam via a pipe
from a water supply heated beneath it.
Under the pressure of the steam escaping
through the nozzles, the sphere would begin to revolve.

Serious research made its most spectacular progress in the fields of astronomy and mathematics. Hipparchus (also of
Alexandria), who could be called the father of Modern Astronomy, discovered the
exact rate of the precession of the equinoxes
(50 seconds a year), a bit of astronomical
information that the great Sir Isaac New-
ton had to rediscover in the seventeenth
century A.D.

THE SCYTHIANS

At the beginning of the first millennium B.C., a horde of nomads called Scyths or Scythians arrived in the south of what is now the Soviet Union, on the shores of the Black Sea and the Caspian Sea; they had been drawn to the west in a great wave of migration, which started in China.

The Scythian tribesmen were excellent horsemen and skilled archers, and the territory they occupied was vast and fertile, rich in pastureland. Some of them settled down and became farmers, but many continued their nomadic life.

The Greek writer Herodotus described the wagons in which they both traveled and lived: ''The smallest have four wheels, others have six; they are sealed with felt and built like houses; some have only one room, others have three. They are impervious to rain, snow, and the winds. The women stay in these wagons, the men accompany them on horseback, followed by their herds of cows and horses. They stay in the same place as long as there is enough fodder to sustain their animals; when all has been eaten, they take themselves somewhere else.''

From the eighth century B.C., the Scythians and Greeks had a good deal of contact with each other. A large number of Greeks visited the Black Sea region, looking for Ukrainian minerals or in search of fishing waters and wheat-growing land. Greek traders, artisans, and goldsmiths found them to be eager clients for articles of gold and silver, and for jewels and wine. Little by little, close links were forged between the two peoples, and a legend grew up that the Scythians were descended from a son of Hercules, a hero called Scythes. One result of these good relations was that the Athenians recruited a corps of Scythian archers to keep order in the city. This corps was the first recorded police force in Europe.

The Scythians buried important warrior chiefs in large tumuli. These were graves 12 to 15 feet deep, covered by a heap of birch and larch wood, logs, and lumps of stone and earth. According to Herodotus, when a chief died, the body was carried about for forty days, followed by a procession of the members of his tribe, who shaved their heads, cut off one ear, and pierced their left hands with arrows as signs of mourning. Then the dead man was buried with his wives, various articles (benches, tables, vases), and precious jewels. The body was placed in a larch wood coffin decorated with applied copper figures.

Scythian art is characterized by its wealth of decoration, almost always depicting animal forms, which are often highly stylized. As hunters and stock breeders, the Scythians' chief form of wealth consisted of wild and domestic animals, and it was these that they chose to fashion in gold and silver. It was only when they came into contact with the Greeks that the Scythians became interested in depicting human beings. A decorative element might consist of a complete animal or just a part; it might be a head, a menacing jaw, or an eye wide open in fear. These images were often adapted to the demands of the overall design. The body would be altered to fit the shape of the object it was used on—a belt buckle, part of a shield, a comb, a vase, a breastplate, or a bracelet.

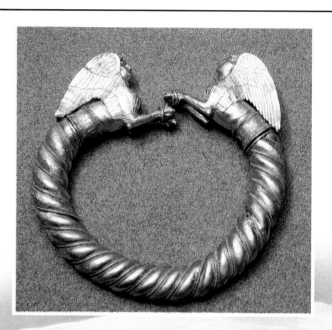

CELTIC CULTURE

In the center of Europe, in the area now occupied by Czechoslovakia, Austria, Germany, and part of Switzerland, a unique civilization began to develop in the first millennium B.C. among a group of peoples whom the Greeks called *Keltoi* (''Celts'').

In the eighth century B.C., anxious to find better agricultural land, the Celts began a series of migrations, some peaceful, some highly aggressive. For three hundred years they launched a succession of invasions toward the south and the west, reaching the Atlantic coast and entering Italy and Spain.

In the fourth century B.C., most of the Celtic tribes, whom the Romans called *Galli* (''Gauls'') had become sedentary. However, a number of tribes continued their migration toward the south and the east of Europe, raiding and pillaging as they went. They sacked Rome in 390 B.C. and set fire to Delphi in 279. Then some of them reached the Adriatic coast, while others occupied Asia Minor, where they founded a kingdom called Galatia (''Land of the Gauls''). The kingdom slowly disappeared, but the name *Galatia* lasted a long time.

With their warlike traditions, wherever they settled, the Gauls retained their taste for battle and were constantly fighting among themselves. Each tribe or people, whether their country was large or small, was governed by a king or magistrate, the *vergobretus*, who was elected by an assembly of warrior-nobles. The aristocrats owned the land and surrounded themselves with slaves and dependents called *ambacti*.

The Gauls lived on the wealth of their agricultural produce and their busy trading activities, which brought them into contact with the Mediterranean cultures. Greek, Etruscan, and Roman traders brought to the Gallic markets their bronze vases, luxurious fabrics, and fine ceramics. The traders visited the Mediterranean ports of Provence in southern France where their ships unloaded olives, oil, and above all, wine, which the Gauls particularly enjoyed.

The Gauls worshiped a number of nature gods in places like woods, groves, and fountains. If anyone fell ill, the tradition was to place near a spring a small carving of the afflicted part of the body in the hope that the god would provide a cure in return. They also worshiped in temples, consisting of a single room surrounded by a covered gallery, near a sacrificial altar and a table of offerings. At major religious ceremonies they sacrificed animals, sometimes in large numbers. And for a long time, it was their practice to sacrifice human beings.

Their religious rituals were in the hands of the Druids, who were both priests and judges. They were universally respected and had immense power, being answerable neither to king nor prince. Their training took twenty years and was purely oral; they were suspicious of written texts, preferring to entrust their secrets to words and memory. Like the Druids, the Gauls used writing very little, and the rare inscriptions that we possess in their language are written in the Greek or Latin alphabet.

The basic material chiefly used by the Gauls was wood: it served as fuel for heating and cooking, and was used as the framework for walls and roofs and for building stockades. With wood the Gauls made farming implements, wagons, riverboats, and seafaring vessels. They also made barrels. Other people in those days were amazed at these complex containers made of narrow planks shaped in a circle.

In battle, Gallic warriors of the first century B.C. used long swords with iron blades and bronze hilts, or they carried spears or javelins. Some soldiers also used bows or slings. Foot soldiers often charged at the same time as the cavalry, who rode small, tough, wiry steeds. The horsemen came from the nobility, the only people who could own horses, and they had full military training. The other soldiers were peasants and artisans, pulled from ordinary life by the demands of war. They used to hurl themselves into the charge in a great yelling, tumultuous mass, with no order or coordination. Most of their enemies were intimidated by this tactic, but it was far from effective against the Roman legions, with their disciplined professional troops. To protect themselves in battle, the Gauls wore bronze or iron helmets that covered their heads and much of their faces. They carried large wood and leather shields, reinforced with metal plates. Some even wore armor of chain mail, a Celtic invention that the Romans adopted. Iron was highly valued in antiquity; since it was stronger than copper or bronze, anyone who could make it had a decided advantage. But it was very laborious to manufacture. Heating iron ore in a kiln produced an unrefined lump that was hammered while hot, heated again, and hammered again, the process being repeated until the metal produced was as pure as possible. From this, ironsmiths forged all kinds of tools—plowshares, axes, forks, scythes, billhooks, saws, knives, wheels, and even iron chains. The Gauls also used iron for all their war weapons and armor—daggers, swords, helmets, and chain mail.

In some parts of northern Gaul, harvesting was done with a mechanical harvester. The Roman author Pliny has left us a description of it, which has been verified by several relief carvings. ''In the vast farmlands of Gaul, a great box with one edge armed with teeth, and carried on two wheels, is pushed through the wheatfields by an ox; the ears of wheat are torn off by the teeth and fall into the box.''

THE BIRTH OF ROME

To the south of Etruria, between the Apennine Mountains and the Mediterranean coast, lies the plain of Latium. This is where the history of Rome began in the eleventh century B.C., when shepherds and farmers came to settle on the hillsides above the left bank of the Tiber River. There they built simple huts of timber, clay, and straw, and began to cultivate vines, olive trees, fig trees, and cereal crops.

Animal husbandry also provided the early Romans with their basic necessities. In addition to these resources, they used timber from the forests to build boats and ships, while salt from the salt lakes at the mouth of the Tiber became the basis of a flourishing trade. Metal, however, had to be obtained from the Etruscans, since the Romans had no supplies of their own.

The first nucleus of the Roman people lived on the Palatine Hill, and new villages grew up on the neighboring Esquiline and Quirinal hills. In the second half of the seventh century B.C., Rome began to develop into a town. The modest thatched huts with their single windows gave way to houses built of masonry with tiled roofs. Between the Palatine and Caelian hills was built the religious and political center, the Forum, paved with flagstones; and the first wooden bridge was built across the Tiber.

The town was in the hands of an aristocracy of rich and powerful families, who ruled over a population of slaves, craftworkers, and farmers. During the seventh century B.C., the use of writing spread, trade became increasingly active, and metallurgy became a widespread industry. Located between several cultures, the town benefited from Greek, Phoenician, and especially Etruscan influences.

Between 616 B.C. and 509 B.C., Etruscan kings ruled over Rome. They installed their palace on the Capitoline and built there a great temple in honor of Jupiter. One of these kings, Servius Tullius, built a rampart of rock around the city; remains of it still exist today. At the end of the fifth century B.C., the Latin aristocracy revolted against the last Etruscan king, Tarquin the Proud, and founded a republic.

The Romans were curious about the origins of their city and had various theories about it. Over the centuries the legend that is described by Virgil in his epic poem the *Aeneid* grew up. The legend is also told by Livy, who wrote a history of Rome ''since the founding of the city.''

The story went that Aeneas, a noble Trojan and son of Venus, fled his country after the Mycenaeans captured Troy. He landed near the mouth of the Tiber, not far from the kingdom of Latinus, and married Latinus's daughter Lavinia. Later his son, Ascanius, founded a city, Alba Longa, on the slopes of the Alban Hills. Several centuries later two descendants of the kings of Alba, twins called Romulus and Remus, were abandoned in their cradle in the waters of the Tiber. A she-wolf kept them alive by suckling them, until they were rescued by shepherds. When they reached manhood, they founded a town on the Palatine Hill. During a quarrel, Romulus killed Remus and became king of the city, which was named after him.

This statue of Romulus and Remus suckled by the she-wolf commemorates the legend of the birth of Rome. The wolf is an Etruscan sculpture of the fifth century B.C. The small bronze figures of the twin brothers were added later by a Renaissance sculptor.

The Latins, the original founders of Rome, cremated their dead and collected the ashes in urns modeled to resemble their houses. Often they added a small human figure in terra cotta and decorated the exterior with models of furniture, dishes, and for dead warriors, bronze weapons. A large terra cotta jar, a dolium, which was used to collect household rubbish, was often used to hold one or several urns. In the seventh century B.C., the custom of cremating the dead was replaced by burial, in imitation of the Greeks and the Etruscans.

In the sixth century B.C., Rome became a huge city, surrounded by a fortified stone wall. The city included the seven hills: the Palatine and Esquiline—the first to be occupied—and the Caelian, Viminal, Quirinal, Capitoline, and Aventine.

THE REPUBLIC AND ITS CONQUESTS

Traditionally it was in 509 B.C. that the Romans drove out the Etruscan king Tarquin the Proud. The newly independent state appointed a Senate of three hundred members from among the noble families of the city, and two consuls, who were elected to serve for a year. By giving the consuls power for such a short period, it was hoped to avoid any risk of returning to a monarchy. Even so, the government of Rome was exclusively in the hands of rich families, the patricians who owned large farming estates from which they drew great wealth. The ordinary people, the plebeians, were excluded from power and provided Rome with its labor force and most of its soldiers. But the plebeians grew tired of their status and decided to claim power for themselves; they even threatened to found a rival city. They won their cause and in 494 B.C. forced the publication of the laws so that all could know their rights. Gradually the plebeians won the right to serve as consul and therefore could enter the Senate. And the initials S.P.Q.R., from the Latin words meaning ''The Senate and the Roman People,'' became the emblem of the Republic.

The city's economic growth, the courage of the legionaries, and the unity of their people made the Romans very powerful, and they launched themselves into the conquest of Italy. They first occupied Etruria, and then seized control of all the Greek colonies in southern Italy and Sicily. After the long-drawn-out Punic Wars, they crushed the power of Carthage. In the first century A.D., the whole area around the Mediterranean was Roman. The small hamlet on the Palatine Hill had given birth to a civilization whose influence extended from the Pillars of Hercules as far as Asia Minor. The defeats inflicted on Rome by the Gauls in 390 B.C. and the Samnites in 321 B.C., together with Hannibal's victories, were no more than faded memories.

In 146 B.C. the capture and destruction of Corinth by the consul Mummius marked the Roman conquest of Greece.

The Romans were primarily land dwellers, soldiers rather than sailors, and for centuries they never ventured on the ocean. The First Punic War forced them to form a military fleet. Copying the Carthaginian and Greek models, they built an armada of 160 ships of war, geared to make the best use of the fighting skills of their legionaries. Traditional tactics consisted of creating confusion among the enemy ships by attacking first with bows and arrows and then ramming the ships. The Romans, however, built their galleys as if they were fighting on land. They provided decks big enough to hold a large number of soldiers, and a movable gangway, called a corvus, with a spike at the end. This could be hooked into the enemy's ship making it easy for the Romans to board. In 260 B.C., off Mylae on the north coast of Sicily, this new tactic met with great success; the Roman foot soldiers won a brilliant victory over the Carthaginian sailors.

ROMAN RELIGION

Roman religion was at first strongly influenced by Etruscan beliefs and rituals. But the Romans soon adopted and assimilated the Greek gods. Zeus, Hera, Athena, and Dionysus were now called Jupiter, Juno, Minerva, and Bacchus. In the Republican era the Romans built temples similar to the Greek ones. They were circular or rectangular, with porticoes topped by pediments. At the entrance of the site, the sacred fire burned, cared for by the Vestal Virgins, who could be buried alive if they broke their vows of chastity. Every family worshiped the household gods—the Lares, Manes, and Penates—spirits, ancestors, and protectors of the domus, the home.

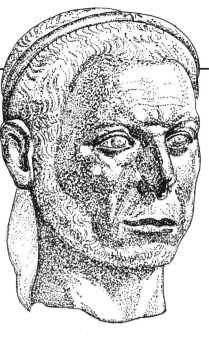

Julius Caesar was born in 102 B.C. into one of the oldest Roman families, the gens Julia (''Julians''), who claimed to be descended from Julus, son of Aeneas, the hero of Troy. Intelligent, brave, and steeped in Greek literature, Caesar embarked on a political career. He was ambitious, claiming that he would prefer to be ''first in a poor village rather than second in Rome.'' He became consul in 59 B.C. and voted for two laws in favor of army veterans and the Roman poor. The following year he became governor of the provinces of northern Italy each side of the Alps, a vital taking-off point for the conquest of Gaul and its riches. At the age of forty-four, the historian Sallust tells us, he was at last granted ''a great command, an army, a new war in which his courage could shine.'' In eight years, 58 to 51 B.C., he conquered Gaul, accumulated a considerable fortune from booty, and became the most popular man with the Roman plebians. He crushed his rival Pom-

pey, and after further victories, which he described proudly in the phrase Veni, vidi, vinci (''I came, I saw, I conquered''), he returned to Rome as its master in 45 B.C. He tightened up the administration of the provinces, founded colonies, and set up the Julian calendar, which we use today, with 365 days, based on the time it takes for the earth to go around the sun. (The previous calendar only had 355 days, so there was a gradual time lag in the seasons.) But Caesar was overly anxious to be recognized as a true king; he went too far and allowed himself to be worshiped as a god. His birth month was dedicated to him and given the name of Julius, from which comes our word July. His ambition brought him many enemies, particularly among the senators who were still loyal to republican ideals. A plot was hatched against him, and he was assassinated on March 15—the Ides of March—in 44 B.C.

THE CENTURY OF AUGUSTUS

After the death of Julius Caesar, conqueror of the Gauls, his grand-nephew and adopted son, Octavian, rose to supreme power in Rome. In 29 B.C., after defeating his chief rival, Mark Anthony, he returned to Rome and was recognized by the senators as first citizen, *princeps* (from which the word *prince* comes). He was careful not to commit the same errors that Caesar had made. He did not try to restore the monarchy, he made sure that the laws of the Republic were observed, and he did not interfere with the Senate or the traditional powers of the magistrates. But in fact, he held all the power that mattered. He was the *imperator*, the commander in chief of the army; he was chief pontiff, custodian of Roman religion; and he had the tribunician power, the right to veto the Senate's decisions.

The senators accepted the situation; in 27 B.C., showered with honor and riches by their new master, they bestowed on him the title of *Augustus* ("Venerable"), which until then had only been applied to places and things dedicated to the gods. Twenty-five years later, he was called Father of the Country. By then, Augustus had become sovereign of the Mediterranean, in fact if not in name. After long periods of civil war, he had restored peace and order to Italy and the Mediterranean region. The empire had been enlarged by new conquests. There was a well-established administration, and the budget and finances had been reorganized.

On his death, Augustus was proclaimed divine; the ceremony of apotheosis was held, making him a god, and altars and temples were dedicated to him. Tiberius, whom he had nominated, acceded to power without opposition. The Republic was truly dead, superseded by an empire that was to last for over four centuries! Tiberius began his reign along the lines laid down by Augustus but ended it as a tyrant. After him, Caligula, Claudius, and Nero, in particular, behaved like despots, often with great cruelty. The next dynasty, the Flavians, notably Vespasian and Titus, restored the good name of *emperor*, only to be followed by Domitian, who governed very badly. Despite all these problems the empire stood firm. Its frontiers were well protected against outside threats, and all the palace intrigues did not affect the *Pax Romana* ("Roman Peace"), which prevailed in the provinces.

Augustus lived on in the memory of the Romans as an extraordinary figure, a man protected by the gods. This view of him can be found in a text by the historian Suetonius, who wrote *Lives of the Caesars* in the second century A.D.: "Augustus was exceptionally handsome. Whether he spoke or whether he was silent, his face expressed an equal serenity, a total tranquillity. His eyes were clear and shining; he was well pleased if any man who looked at him closely had soon to turn away his gaze, as if to avoid the blinding rays of the sun."

Octavian (Gaius Octavius) was born in Rome in 63 B.C., son of Octavius, governor of Macedonia, and Julius Caesar's niece Atia. After his father's death the young Octavian was adopted by his great-uncle and followed him on his military campaigns in Spain. Caesar made him his heir, and he took the name Gaius Julius Caesar Octavianus. After Caesar's murder, he swore to avenge him. Having achieved this aim by eliminating Mark Anthony, he was sole master in Rome. Upon his death he named his son-in-law Tiberius as his successor, passing on to him the empire he had created during his thirty years in power.

The triumphal arch is a specific Roman architectural feature. Originally, at the end of the second century B.C., monumental timber gateways were put up to welcome generals who had won the right to the title imperator. Later, these gateways were built as grand stone monuments. Under the empire, arches dedicated to emperors sprang up in almost all the Roman cities, showing that they belonged to Rome. One was the arch pictured here, built at Thuburbo Majus, in present-day Tunisia.

During the Republican period the word triumphus simply signified a victorious general's return to Rome at the head of his troops, acclaimed by the crowd, and his visit to the temple on the Capitol to give thanks to the gods. In Caesar's time the ceremony took its definitive form as a highly organized victory parade. The participants set out from the Field of Mars and arrived at the Forum, where they took the Sacred Way up to the Capitol. At the head of the procession came the senators and magistrates, followed by trumpeters; behind them, trophies and possessions captured from the enemy were displayed on biers or carts, accompanied by placards showing where they came from. Next came the captives, the defeated kings and leaders, tied or in chains, walking on foot or put on show in chariots. The conquering leader was dressed to look like Jupiter, in a purple tunic and a toga decorated with gold stars. He wore a laurel wreath and held a scepter in one hand and a laurel branch in the other.

THE ROMAN EMPIRE IN THE SECOND CENTURY A.D.

The second century A.D. was the most brilliant period in the history of the Roman Empire, which by that time stretched from the North Sea to the Sahara and from the Atlantic Ocean to the Black Sea.

Its forty-three provinces covered an area equal to ten times that of modern-day France, with several tens of millions of inhabitants. There were towns everywhere built in stone and marble, while colonies for army veterans grew up in conquered lands. Many towns were built according to set plans with straight roads crossing each other at right angles. The resulting blocks which lay between these roads were called insulae ("islands"). The main north-south thoroughfare was called the *cardo* and the east-west thoroughfare, the *decumanus*. At the spot where these two streets crossed was an area called the *forum*. An area similar in many ways to the Greek *agora*, the forum was essentially the town's business district. In a forum could be found temples, market buildings, seats of government, and basilicas (large buildings used as law courts and places for public assembly). The most prosperous cities also took pride in putting up buildings for leisure activities—baths, theaters, odeums, amphitheaters, and circuses.

The wealth of the empire seemed limitless. The provinces of Egypt, North Africa, and Gaul supplied wheat, wine, and oil. Lead, iron, copper, and silver came from Spain and the Danube region, tin from the British Isles, luxury goods from the East, pottery from Gaul, and animals for circus games from Africa and the German forests. A constant flow of all these goods arrived at Ostia, the busy port of Rome.

All this wealth meant that Rome could supply the service of the *annona*, a free distribution of cereals, meat, fruit, and vegetables. The empire profited from its thriving commercial activities by taxing markets and the sale of salt, and by imposing customs and toll duties; this swelled the revenues from the taxes already paid by the provinces and large landowners.

Gradually townspeople all over the empire acquired Roman citizenship, with the same privileges as the people of Rome. Citizenship gave them special legal rights and freed them from certain duties, and in many provinces, citizens could aspire to a seat in the Roman Senate.

As if to illustrate the unity of the empire, Trajan, the first great emperor of the second century, was born in Spain. He extended Roman power by conquering the Dacians on the banks of the Danube and the Parthians in the East. His adopted son, Hadrian, who ruled from 117 to 138, aimed to strengthen the unity of the empire's provinces and to consolidate their defenses. He traveled widely through the empire and was responsible for many new buildings, including his beautiful villa at Tivoli, outside Rome. His successor, Antoninus Pius, spent twenty-three years in office simply governing the flourishing empire, without ever leaving Rome. But Marcus Aurelius, who succeeded him, had to deal with many problems, including the threat of the Germanic tribes who were breaking through the Danube frontiers, bringing an end to the *Pax Romana*. In 180, during one of his campaigns against the invaders, Marcus Aurelius died of the plague. With him, the most brilliant period of Roman history came to an end.

The Emperor Hadrian wanted to protect the borders of the empire. He strengthened the northern frontier between Scotland and England (then called Britannia) by building the famous fortification known as Hadrian's Wall, between 122 and 126 B.C. It was a continuous wall crossing the whole island from east to west, from the Tyne to the Solway. It was reinforced every mile with turrets and small forts (mile castles). There were permanent camps at intervals, which included barracks, food reserves, baths, a sanctuary, and resident craftworkers to look after supplies and maintain weapons. Large ditches completed the defense, while a well-maintained road enabled troops to move about at speed. Large sections of Hadrian's Wall still exist.

Ostia stands at the mouth (ostium means "mouth" in Latin) of the Tiber; at the beginning of the fourth century B.C., the Romans made it a thriving port. Here all the produce of the empire arrived. Around the central square, Corporation Square, stood sixty-four offices representing commercial organizations all over the Roman world. Merchant vessels were often small single-masted tubs, with high prows, square sails, and two steering oars.

Roman religion was very tolerant toward the religious beliefs of conquered nations, so long as the nations agreed to render homage to Rome and the emperor. This ''Imperial Cult'' forged a powerful bond between the emperor and his subjects. The worship of Rome and the emperor was like the worship of the other gods; a ceremony was held in front of the temple, around an altar at which sacrifices were made. The priests often sacrificed animals whose entrails were then examined for omens by diviners called haruspices. Some Roman temples were truly impressive, like this temple to Bacchus at Baalbek in Lebanon, built in the second century A.D. It had forty-two columns nearly 65 feet high.

THE ROMAN LEGIONS

T he Roman army was the key factor in the conquests of the Republic and the empire. Servius Tullius, king of Rome in the sixth century B.C., was the first to organize the army according to social rank. The wealthiest citizens formed the cavalry. The infantry was divided into five classes. In the first class, the heavy infantry, each soldier carried a sword, lance, helmet, and shield, and wore a metal breastplate and greaves. The next three classes were formed of soldiers with lightweight equipment, and the fifth was composed of slingers.

The army remained unchanged until the early days of the Republic but was modified after the Gauls captured Rome in 390 B.C. At that time a new tactic was adopted. In battle the men in the two front lines carried heavy javelins, *pila*, which they threw at the enemy; then they unsheathed their swords and engaged in hand-to-hand fighting. Behind them advanced the third-line soldiers, the *triarii*, who carried lances.

At the end of the second century B.C., Marius, who had defeated a wave of Germanic invaders, the Cimbri and the Teutoni, set up a truly professional army. Every soldier now signed on for a specific period (ten years for the cavalry, sixteen for the foot soldiers); they then qualified as veterans and could be given territory to colonize.

At full strength a legion consisted of six thousand men divided into ten cohorts. There were three maniples to a cohort, and each maniple was made up of two centuries (one hundred men). In overall command was a general assisted by military tribunes. Each legion also included administrative services, a sanitary service, and *immunes*, specialists in building siege engines.

The other strengths of the legion lay in its marching order, the *agmen*, which enabled it to move about without fear of surprise attack, and in its expertise in building fortified camps. At a stopping point, part of the troop would keep watch while patrols went off in search of forage. The remaining men would dig ditches and embankments topped with palisades.

Every legionary was equipped to look after himself and take part in setting up camp. He carried cooking utensils, a water bottle, a bag for personal belongings, and various tools—a pick, an ax, a spade, rope, a basket, and bedding.

THE ART OF THE SIEGE

Roman soldiers had developed to a fine art the skills of fortifying their camps and besieging enemy strongholds. During the Gallic Wars, Julius Caesar had to build a large number of fortified camps for his legions, and he had to besiege many Gallic fortresses. Of all his building works, the most spectacular were carried out at the siege of Alesia; Caesar's descrip-

tion of them has been verified by excavations. Around Mount Auxois, on which the fortress of Alesia stood, the legions built a complete circle of two earthen ramparts, topped by palisades and towers, and protected by ditches and quantities of traps. The defenses were so strong that neither the besieged nor the huge army that came to their aid could break them down.

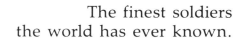

This highly efficient helmet was the result of a series of designs originally inspired by Hellenistic and Gallic models. This one is called the "Imperial Gallic" or "Jockey Cap," because of the large visor over the front of the head. The face was protected by two hinged cheekpieces that were fastened under the chin, while the back of the neck was fully covered.

The onager ("donkey") was a siege machine that could fling 130-pound rocks over distances of about 200 yards.

On campaigns, legionaries had a lot to carry. In addition to their helmets, from the first century A.D. onward, they were also protected by flexible metal armor worn over a wool tunic. During the Gallic Wars they began wearing breeches or trousers in regions where the climate was harsh. Shields were oval or rectangular and were always curved to give better protection; they were made of wood covered with leather and trimmed with metal. Weapons consisted of a heavy javelin, a pilum; a short sword, the gladius; and a dagger. Soldiers were shod with stout leather sandals with studded soles. Discipline was very harsh, aimed at ensuring total obedience. Punishments for transgressions ranged from heavy duties to flogging. The worst crime was cowardice in battle, leading to the death of soldiers; for this the punishment was death by beating or stoning.

LIFE IN ROME

In the second century A.D., Rome had nearly a million inhabitants. The rich dwellings of the aristocracy and the emperors' palaces stood close to the communal apartment houses that were several stories high, which Trajan limited to 60 feet. The apartment houses were hastily built by the thousands, "supported only by beams as long and thin as flutes," wrote Juvenal; sometimes they fell down, and they were an easy prey for the fires that periodically swept through the capital.

The Forum, marketplaces, and temples were favorite meeting places for the cosmopolitan population, who came from all the provinces of the vast empire. Every religion could be found there and all kinds of goods; there could be heard every language spoken by the nations who had been conquered over the centuries, from the British Isles to the Arabian deserts, from Germania to the Sahara.

Rome had become a parasitic city, living on the generosity of powerful citizens who provided food and entertainment. Tens of thousands of Romans flocked to the public baths, amphiteaters, circuses, and theaters. There was a constant and varied choice of spectacles. Audiences of 250,000 could be seated in the *Circus Maximus* ("Large Circus"), where the charioteers had to race seven times around the track. In the time of the Flavians, up to a hundred races were held there every day! And the Colosseum, built between A.D. 72 and 82, could hold 50,000 people. When it was opened, the Emperor Domitian put on a hundred days of games, during which 9,000 animals died and 2,000 gladiators were killed.

ROMAN AQUEDUCTS

The city of Rome needed enormous amounts of water. In the third century A.D., this was supplied by eleven aqueducts, which carried in over 35 million cubic feet daily. If the city's population is estimated at a million, that means there were 264 gallons available per person a day (this is double what a town supplies today). One of the most impressive feats of Roman engineering is the 6½ miles of stone arches supporting two superimposed aqueducts, the Aqua Claudia and the Anio Novus, which combined water brought from two different sources in a single overhead channel. When the water reached the city, it passed through decanting chambers, where impurities were filtered out. It was then carried underground in lead pipes to the city supply points, public or private fountains and baths.

The Forum was the center of Rome. It was built in a once marshy valley, drained during the reigns of the last Etruscan kings, and lying between the Capitoline, Palatine, and Esquiline hills. The senators met in the Curia, a massive rectangular building. Close by were the rostra, platforms used by political orators. On the west side rose the Basilica Julia and on the east the Basilica Aemilia, in front of which passed the Via Sacra ("Sacred Way"), the route taken by processions and triumphant warriors. The Forum also included numerous temples, colonnades, and porticoes, and the House of the Vestals, the guardians of the city's sacred fire. Here too were the oldest and most sacred parts of the city, including the Umbilicus Urbis ("Navel of Rome"), which marked the theoretical center of the city, and the Milliarum Aureum ("Golden Milestone"), which gave the distances between Rome and the towns of the empire. In the early morning the first traders would set up their stalls. Gradually the areas around the Forum would come to life, filling up with crowds of the curious, idlers, beggars, and visitors, all seeking food and entertainment.

POMPEII

Buried under the lava of Mount Vesuvius in A.D. 79, the small city of Pompeii has preserved unique evidence about daily life in the days of ancient Rome.

Pompeii had from twelve thousand to fifteen thousand inhabitants; it lay in the heart of rich countryside that was scattered with farms owned by a rural population of about three thousand to five thousand.

The city was governed by leading families of bankers, landowners, industrialists, and merchants. Around this rich class revolved an underprivileged population of slaves and free men. Though poor, they were not wretched; they could earn enough to buy bread and basic foodstuffs, which were not expensive. In addition, the privileged classes were generous; it was in their interest to spend some of their wealth on beautifying the city and building places where people could gather and enjoy themselves, such as the public baths, the forum, and the amphitheater.

The rich owned very large houses, whose living rooms faced an inner court. In the center of the court, they had peaceful flower gardens, where pools and fountains glimmered, sheltered from the summer heat and the noises of the town.

By contrast, in the town streets, shopkeepers lived above their stores. Other people rented a room or two, where they slept on rough matting on the floor. The real home of the crowd, the humble and lowly people, was the street; cluttered with traders' stalls, it was busy from morning till night. Inns and taverns provided snacks of vegetable or fish soups and raw vegetables, washed down with watered wine, to fill the gap before the main meal, the *cena*, in the evening.

"THE STREET OF ABUNDANCE"

As in all the cities, tradespeople in Pompeii congregated in particular streets. Archaeologists have named one "The Street of Abundance." It contained the largest number of shops. Just about every house on either side of this long thoroughfare contained one or two businesses, consisting of a salesroom opening onto the street, with a counter at the front, and some small living rooms. The furniture and inscriptions in the houses have enabled them to be identified; there were several shops, grain and dry goods merchants, a hardware store, a laundry, a lamp maker, a weaver, three inns, and even some private baths.

In one of the inns of Pompeii, archaeologists have found a
personal inscription engraved on a wall: Oliva condita XVII
K novembris ("I put the olives to pickle on the 17 of the
month of November"). On another wall a satisfied customer
wrote: Futui cauponam ("I slept with the maidservant").
There was so much graffiti of this kind scrawled on the walls
that someone else wrote on three separate walls of Pompeii:
"I wonder, O wall, that you do not crash under the weight
of this stupid trash!" But it was not stupidity that knocked
Pompeii down; it was the devastating eruption of its neighbor, Mount Vesuvius.

Taken by surprise when
Vesuvius erupted in terrify-
ing fashion in A.D. 79, on
August 24, all the Pom-
peians who failed to flee at
the first signs were killed,
suffocated by ash, poison
fumes, and the burning heat.
The dust hardened so closely around perishable objects
and human and animal
corpses that their contours
remained after they had
decayed. Liquid plaster was
blown into the hollow spaces
thus created; when this
hardened, their tragic shapes
were reproduced in lifelike
fashion.

THE REMAINS OF
A CIVILIZATION

Today, from Holland to Libya, from Portugal to Syria, from Hungary to Jordan, from Morocco to Romania, the remains of the Roman Empire survive in stone ruins. Broken pillars, pieces of wall, fallen statues, and crumbling mosaics can be found everywhere. After twenty centuries of history, these traces of Roman civilization can be read like a well-worn book. Yet the domination of Rome did not change the life-styles of the different countries, regions, and provinces.

In places where civilizations had existed for centuries, like Greece, Asia Minor, and Egypt, the Roman conquest affected people's way of life very little. The local architecture and town building styles, already flourishing when the invaders arrived, continued to predominate. In Roman times the Egyptians built their Nile Valley temples in the Egyptian style, and the Greeks used Greek techniques to build their temples in Caria and Lycia. Although Latin was the official language of Byzantium in the sixth century A.D., Greek continued to be spoken and written all over the eastern world until the Arab and Ottoman invasions.

By contrast, in regions like North Africa, Spain, and Gaul, the Roman influence made such a powerful impact on language, architecture, town planning, and technology that it is not always easy to find evidence of the local cultures that existed there before.

Despite these differences, the monuments erected by Rome to affirm its prestige and impress its subject nations provided most people not just with imposing architecture but with a completely new experience of comfort, education, and leisure activities.

The Romans built a vast network of roads that could be used in all seasons, providing a means of fast travel for their legions and creating trade and cultural links throughout the empire. No obstacle could defeat their engineers; they could build roads on steep, winding mountainsides, bore tunnels through mountains, and elevate viaducts over ravines and rivers. Surfaces were regularly repaired, relay posts were set up, and the roads competed with sea travel for the ever-increasing amount of commercial, military, personal, and cultural traffic. Under Augustus a particularly modern institution was created, a kind of mail service called the cursus publicus. By this system dispatches could be carried anywhere in the empire, using fast, light carriages and relays of horses. The historian Suetonius tells us: "Augustus had the habit of adding to all his letters the exact hour of the day or night when he sent them."

Hundreds of Roman roads have been listed: they are known through archaeological remains, such as milestones; through aerial photography; and from ancient and medieval records, such as the Antonine Itinerary, a list of routes for soldiers or travelers, and the Peutinger Table, a twelfth-century copy probably based on a third-century map of the world. In the towns and suburbs and on particularly important sections of the route, the roads were paved. Top speed on Roman roads could not have been more than 95 miles a day. The mail covered 50 miles in twenty-four hours, and an average traveler, 28 miles.

THE ROMAN GAMES

All the cities of the empire wanted to emulate Rome in owning a theater, an odeum for musical contests, a circus for chariot races, and an amphitheater for gladiatorial contests. Only the richest cities could afford such buildings; many of the ruins of these are standing today. There, spectacles took place, which

Seneca has described for us: "In the morning, men are delivered to lions and bears; at midday they are delivered to the spectators. When one has killed, he has to stand up to another to be killed. . . . For the combatants there is only one outcome—death."

In the Roman world, laws, state decisions, important events, and inaugurations were engraved on stones called stelae, which were put in public places so that everyone could take note of them. This stela is inscribed with a decree by the Emperor Vespasian, appointing a tribune called Suedius Clemens to deal with a territorial problem that had arisen in Pompeii. It concerned some local people, victims of an earthquake, who had provisionally set up home on land allocated as a burial ground.

The Latin language played a tremendous part in unifiying the empire. Although Greek remained the language of education for a long time, Latin was used for government acts, laws, decrees, imperial edicts, correspondence of the imperial offices, and inscriptions on monuments. Writers, historians, and playwrights also used Latin, and their works circulated throughout the empire. They included the historians Sallust, Suetonius, Livy, and Tacitus; the poets Virgil and Horace; the novelists Petronius and Apuleius; and many other writers, such as Seneca, Pliny, and Juvenal.

One of the building methods used throughout the Roman Empire was the alternation of layers of stones and layers of bricks. Walls built in this way were extremely solid and can be found today at a large number of sites. The one shown here is at Jublains in Mayenne, western France.

THE END OF AN EMPIRE

T he vast size and complex organization of the Roman Empire made it extremely vulnerable. Any external threat or internal dispute could endanger its very existence; and that is what happened, starting in the third century.

The ambitious army generals, sure of support from their armies, began to jockey for power. Whole provinces seceded, like Gaul, where a Gallic emperor announced that he no longer recognized Roman authority and set up a capital at Trier on the Rhine. At the other end of the empire, the great city of Palmyra in Syria made itself into an independent principality.

Everywhere there was mounting insecurity. Piracy was revived in the Mediterranean. Trade became shaky, and money lost its value. In town and country, people experienced famine. And the Germanic tribes began to force their way through the frontiers.

In 270, when Aurelian came to power, the situation improved for a time. The empire recovered its unity, but the danger of invasion was still so great that people fortified their towns. A strong wall was built around Rome itself, the first since the beginning of the Republic.

At the end of the century, Diocletian, son of a Dalmatian freeman, became emperor. Faced with insoluble organizational problems, he tried setting up a tetrarchy, a fourfold division of the empire in which the power was shared between two joint and two subordinate emperors (Augustuses and Caesars). But this cumbersome system did not survive him. Diocletian himself abdicated in 305 and retired to his fine palace at Salona (present-day Split) in Dalmatia.

In 312, at the end of a new civil war, Constantine, son of one of the tetrarchs, took over the empire. One of his first acts was to recognize Christianity as a permitted religion in the empire; up until then, Christians had suffered frequent persecutions. He decided to transfer the capital of the empire farther east and chose Byzantium as the seat of power, giving it his name—*Constantinople*.

During the decades following Constantine's death, the Roman world was wracked by constant internal strife, schisms, and short-lived reunifications. In 379 the Emperor Theodosius I succeeded in unifying the empire for the last time. The price he paid was to enlist in the Roman armies a mass of barbarians, whose task was to push other barbarians back from the frontiers! At his death in 395, he left the empire to be shared between his two sons. The eldest, Arcadius, was given the Eastern Empire, ruling at Constantinople, and the younger, Honorius, ruled the Western Empire from Milan. The Eastern Empire lasted for over a thousand years more, but the Western Empire was brought to an end by invasions of the Germanic and other tribes in the fifth century.

In 410, Alaric, king of the Visigoths, seized Rome. His death, like that of Attila several years later, saved Italy for the time being, but the Western Empire was shattered by wave after wave of invaders, and it finally fell completely into the hands of the barbarians. In 476 the Germanic general Odoacer deposed the last emperor, who ironically bore the name of both the founder of Rome and the founder of the Roman Empire: Romulus Augustulus.

A sculpture in red rock (formerly in Byzantium and now in Venice) commemorates the tetrarchs: the two Augustuses and the two Caesars who were supposed to support each other. This highly complicated system, based on a division of responsibilities between four cities (Milan, Nicomedia, Trier, and Sirmium), foundered in anarchy and civil war.

At the end of the third century A.D., barbarian peoples, who had been held back with difficulty along the frontiers, began making bloodthirsty raids into the empire. In the fourth and fifth centuries, Germanic invaders broke through from Greece to Gaul, forcing the local people to leave the countryside and take refuge in cities and fortified towns. But it was the Huns from central Asia, commanded by Attila, who spread the greatest terror through Europe. The great migrations that resulted brought about profound changes in the population and social structure of the West. Gaul was divided among several peoples. The Franks occupied the north of the country; the Alemanni, the northeast; the Burgundians, the plains of the Rhône and the Saône; and the Visigoths, the southwest and Spain. Angles, Saxons, and Jutes landed in the British Isles. The Ostrogoths settled in Italy, and the Vandals in Sardinia, Corsica, and North Africa.

A NEW RELIGION

Roman religion was very formal and was more concerned with ritual than with genuine belief; it provided no comfort for the anguish of the living faced by the mysteries of death. In contrast, the oriental religions offered the hope of an afterlife and attracted more and more believers. The cult of the goddess Isis spread, and so did the worship of Mithras, the Persian sungod, who became very popular among soldiers. There were many purification rituals connected with these new deities; in one Mithraic rite, initiates lay in a coffin-shaped pit while above them the throat of a bull was cut and its blood sprinkled over them. Christianity was also an oriental religion, but its origins and message were very different from those of the other religions. It began and developed in Judea, where a large number of Jews were hoping for the coming of a savior, the Messiah promised by the Bible. To many of those who knew him, Jesus Christ seemed to be this awaited savior. Arrested, condemned, and crucified by the Romans, according to his disciples he rose again three days later. After his death, those who remained faithful to the teachings and message of Jesus Christ called themselves Christians. Some Christians, including all the disciples who had believed in Jesus from the start, traveled the Mediterranean to spread the gospel, the good news of the son of God come down to Earth to deliver people from their sins and to offer them eternal life. Gradually a new religion took form. To its eastern and Jewish origins were added Greco-Roman influences, particularly through the leadership of Paul of Tarsus, a Greek-born Roman converted to Christianity. In the second and third centuries, Christianity took root throughout the empire. The Christians, with their total belief in one God, refused to worship the emperor and became involuntary outcasts in the Roman Empire. They suffered terrible persecutions but remained unshaken in their faith, which was based on loving one's neighbor, nonviolence, and respect for God's commandments. The Christians became more and more numerous, particularly in the towns, and they organized themselves under priests and bishops. The most important, the bishop of Rome, became the pope of all Christendom. People of all classes were converted, and Christianity became the main religion of the Roman world. At the beginning of the fourth century, before his own deathbed conversion, the Emperor Constantine recognized the preeminence of this religion, which had begun three centuries before.

BYZANTIUM

The Byzantine civilization is too often thought of as simply a branch of the dying Roman Empire. But that is to ignore the 1,123 years between 330, when Constantinople was consecrated, and 1453, when it was captured by the Turks.

Around 660 B.C., Greek colonists from Megara and Argos had founded the town of Byzantium on the banks of the Bosporus. A thousand years later, Constantine the Great, ruler of the Roman Empire in 324, chose it as his capital, under the name *Constantinople*. With its unique position between Europe and Asia, the town underwent enormous expansion and took over the Roman heritage after the fall of Rome in the fifth century A.D. The Emperor Justinian and his general Belisarius even conquered back a good deal of lost territory, but they were unable to establish an empire like that of Augustus. They had to leave a major part of Spain to the Visigoths, Gaul to the Franks, and England to the Britons, Angles, and Saxons. However, the Adriatic and most of the Mediterranean became Byzantine waters.

Constantinople, like Rome, was filled with magnificent buildings; there was a large forum, a huge circus—the hippodrome could hold 100,000 spectators—and several palace complexes for the emperor's use. Above all, now that Christianity was the official religion, hundreds of churches were built.

The city was dominated by the dome of St. Sophia; this supreme marvel of Byzantine architecture, founded by the Emperor Justinian in 537, affirmed the brilliance and vitality of the new empire.

The clergy, proud of their achievements and of the greatness of Byzantium, became increasingly important. In 381 an Ecumenical Council held at Constantinople proclaimed the Byzantine Patriarch to be equal with the pope of Rome. Later, rivalry between the two led to a complete split between the Roman Catholic Church and the Orthodox Church.

The people of Constantinople had plenty of pleasures, too; in the sixth century there were numerous public baths and four theaters, where a large number of entertainments were held, compensating for the disappearance of the bloodthirsty Roman games. Starting in the reign of Constantine, there were 179 public holidays a year, with theatrical spectacles on 101 of them.

But the most wildly popular form of entertainment was the horse-and-chariot racing in the hippodrome; as the Byzantine saying went, "St. Sophia belongs to God, the palace to the emperor, and the hippodrome to the people."

Byzantium had a considerable and lasting influence on culture; to the east and south, the Moslem world drew on it for centuries in the building and decoration of their mosques and palaces; to the north and west, the whole Slavic world became impregnated with its religion, writing, and architectural and artistic styles. And for the Western world, it provided a vast pool of knowledge accumulated over the centuries of Greek and Roman culture.

The Byzantine emperor, the basileus, carried on as a Christian the role of the pagan emperor of Rome, presenting himself as a divine being and surrounding himself with incredible luxury and pomp. Two thrones stood in the great hall of the palace, where he received ambassadors: the emperor sat on one throne; the other was empty, reserved for Christ. On ceremonial occasions the emperor wore a cloak covered in costly embroideries and sparkling jewels; he wore bracelets, pendants, and collars of gold and diamonds, as well as a crown topped with a cross. The throne of Byzantium was not hereditary. These emperors, who likened themselves to gods and were untouchable, held power because they had been elected by the Senate, the army, and the people. Anyone with courage, a powerful personality, or a gift for intrigue could try his chance. Leo I had been a butcher; Justin I, a soldier born a peasant; Phocas, a centurion; Michael III, a servant; and Basil I, a slave.

The magnificent church of St. Sophia was built by the emperor Justinian I. Between A.D. 532 and 537, ten thousand laborers worked on it nonstop, using a huge variety of luxurious materials: marble of every hue, brought from all corners of the empire; silver; gold; ivory; and precious fabrics. The dome above the center of the church is a masterpiece of technology; it spans 107 feet and contains countless windows through which light floods into the building. At the opening of this sumptuous monument, Justinian raised his hands to heaven and cried: "Glory to God who has judged me worthy to accomplish such a work! Oh, Solomon, I have defeated you!" After the Ottoman conquest in 1453, St. Sophia was turned into a mosque.

By the end of the second century A.D., Roman families had fewer and fewer children, and illustrations of young mothers looking after their children at that time are rare. Especially in the richest classes, mothers with three to five children were regarded as outstanding, worthy of honor and distinction.

THE WIFE AND FAMILY IN ANTIQUITY

In ancient Greece and Rome, families were never very big. To avoid having too many mouths to feed or having to split up inheritances, couples had few children, and it was up to the father to decide whether a new baby would be accepted or rejected. In Rome a father had eight days to make this decision if the child was a girl, nine days if it was a boy. If the father refused to accept a child into the family, it could be abandoned in a public place. In Athens an abandoned child would be exposed in a clay receptacle on the steps of a temple, and in Rome it would be left on a rubbish heap. Sometimes people rescued abandoned infants, not out of kindness of the heart but so that they could employ the children as slaves when they were old enough. The practice of abandoning newborn babies primarily affected girls, for male heirs were held in higher regard. "One always brings up a son oneself, even if one is poor; a daughter is exposed, even if one is rich," wrote a Greek poet. It was not until Christianity became the official religion of the empire that this legal form of infanticide was abolished, in A.D. 374.

Naming a child

In Athens, when a boy baby was accepted, he was carried around the family altar in his parent's arms. A few days later, family and friends would gather at a banquet, where the child would be given his name. To distinguish him from others with the same name, he would also be given the name of his father and of the *deme*, the district he was born in—for example, Alcibiades, son of Clinias of the deme of Samsonide.

In Rome a boy child who was recognized and accepted was sprinkled with water in ritual purification; then a *bulla*, a small locket full of lucky charms, was placed around his neck. Boys' names had three parts—the *tria nomina*—consisting of a first name (*praenomen*), a family name (*nomen*), and a surname (*cognomen*). The *praenomen* was taken from distant ancestors to whom the newborn was related; there were only eighteen possibilities, of which the most common were Gaius, Lucius, and Titus. The *nomen* ended in *-ius* and was the family name. The *cognomen* distinguished different branches of the same family. A famous example is the name of Gaius Julius Caesar. In Athens, like Rome, having one's own name was an exclusively male prerogative. In Rome, girls were only given a feminine version of the name of the *gens*, the family in its widest, tribal sense—for example, Cornelia and Livia.

Head of a hooded woman, possibly Pericles' companion Aspasia of Miletus. Roman copy of an original Greek bronze of the fifth century B.C.

In the Roman Republic, couples had a reputation for being united; but under the empire, divorce became increasingly widespread. For a long time, divorce was always initiated by the man, but little by little, women too acquired the right to divorce. Seneca asserted that women no longer counted years by the names of consuls, as was customary, but by the names of their different husbands!

The gynaeceum

In both Greece and Rome, women had no political role and were treated as perpetual minors. A girl was dependent on her father, a wife on her husband, and a widow on her son or on a guardian appointed in her husband's will. In the *Odyssey* this is what Telemachus says to his mother, Penelope: "Go within your chamber, supervise the spinning and weaving, order your servants to go about their duties; speech is the business of men, and above all mine, I who am master in this palace." In wealthy families the Greek wife spent her life enclosed in the *gynaeceum*, the women's quarters. There was no need for bolted doors or barred windows; women were kept in by the power of custom, because going out alone brought dishonor. They only went out accompanied, on special occasions such as city festivals or family

events. Women did not choose their own husbands; a husband was chosen by the father or guardian of a woman. At the betrothal ceremony preceding a wedding, sacrifices were offered to the household gods, and in Rome and the Roman Empire, the fiancé gave his bride-to-be a ring, which she put on the ring finger of her left hand. This custom, which we follow today, goes back a very long way. The Latin writer Aulus Gellius tells us: "When a human corpse is opened up and dissected, as practiced by the Egyptians, a very fine nerve can be found leading from the ring finger to the heart. It is thought appropriate to honor this finger with the ring, rather than any other, because of the close connection uniting it with the most important organ."

Hetaerae and concubines

A small number of women, usually slaves or free foreigners, had the advantage of coming under a different law in ancient cities; these women included *hetaerae* ("superior courtesans") and concubines. They escaped from the ignorance and isolation of the *gynaeceum* and were allowed to attend male gatherings, where they could listen to philosophical discussions and poetical discourses. In this way some of them acquired a literary and musical education that made them very desirable companions. One of the most famous was Aspasia, an intelligent and remarkably cultivated concubine whom Pericles loved dearly—to the extent of opposing laws that he himself had promulgated!

Sparta was the only city of antiquity in which girls were brought up exactly like boys. They were trained to be brave and strong through physical exercise, and they shared a number of activities with the boys. Sparta wanted its warriors to have courageous wives, with no weaknesses, who would provide the state with vigorous children.

After the Hellenistic period, women's position improved under the Roman Empire. They were still excluded from politics, but they played an essential role in family life; their title, *matrona*, was accompanied by a genuine authority. At important gatherings and meals, a wife could be present beside her husband (as had been the case with the Etruscans). Wives were asked for their advice and often gave it with conviction and decisiveness. And the influence of some of the empresses on their husbands should never be underestimated. Some that had powerful personalities were Augustus's wife, Livia; Trajan's wife, Plotina; Antoninus's wife, Faustina; and their daughter, the young wife of Marcus Aurelius.

THE WANDERINGS OF ULYSSES

Very few texts by Greek authors have survived the implacable march of the centuries to the present day. In ancient Greece, literary works were written by hand on papyrus scrolls, and copies were made so that the work could be both preserved and widely read. For two thousand years of Greek, Roman, Byzantine, and medieval history, some works were thus copied and recopied: the ones that survived were those that continued to interest the public despite changes over time in tastes, beliefs, and philosophical and religious ideas. Only a tiny proportion of writings have come through this filter; they have also had to contend with censorship and destruction. We know that there were at least 150 writers of tragedy in Greece, but we only have the literary remnants of three of them—Aeschylus, Sophocles, and Euripides. And of the three hundred works they wrote collectively, we only possess thirty-three complete plays!

Immortal Homer

In the contest for immortality, the laurels have to go to Homer, whose two long epic poems, the *Iliad* and the *Odyssey*, seem to have crossed the time barrier without drastic cuts or alterations. Homer's works had the same cultural importance for the Hellenic world as the Bible has had for the Judeo-Christian world. This man, whom the Greeks called "the poet," achieved this victory because of the huge popularity of his thousands of lines of verse. No library of antiquity, the Middle Ages, or the

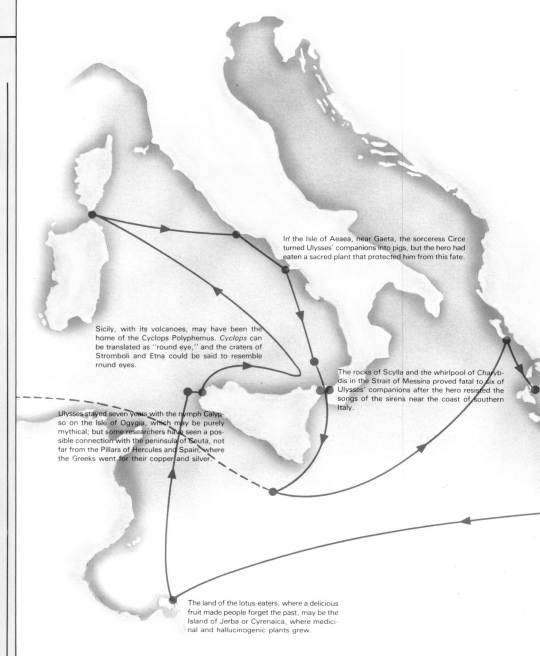

In the Isle of Aeaea, near Gaeta, the sorceress Circe turned Ulysses' companions into pigs, but the hero had eaten a sacred plant that protected him from this fate.

Sicily, with its volcanoes, may have been the home of the Cyclops Polyphemus. *Cyclops* can be translated as "round eye," and the craters of Stromboli and Etna could be said to resemble round eyes.

The rocks of Scylla and the whirlpool of Charybdis in the Strait of Messina proved fatal to six of Ulysses' companions after the hero resisted the songs of the sirens near the coast of southern Italy.

Ulysses stayed seven years with the nymph Calypso on the Isle of Ogygia, which may be purely mythical; but some researchers have seen a possible connection with the peninsula of Ceuta, not far from the Pillars of Hercules and Spain, where the Greeks went for their copper and silver.

The land of the lotus-eaters, where a delicious fruit made people forget the past, may be the Island of Jerba or Cyrenaica, where medicinal and hallucinogenic plants grew.

Renaissance was complete without the works of Homer. Among all the papyrus fragments found by archaeologists in Egypt over the last few decades, over half relate to Homer's tales. If a Greek living in Egypt after Alexander's conquest owned a few books—a few papyrus scrolls—the chances are one in two that they were Homer's poems. Homer lived around the middle of the eighth century B.C. He was almost certainly born on the Isle of Chios and died on the Isle of Ios, in the Cyclades. He may have belonged to the brotherhood of bards who chanted epic poems while accompanying themselves on the lyre. They went from town to town and palace to pal-

ace, visiting noble families and providing entertainment at their festivities. But Homer was not just a recitalist: when he composed the *Iliad* and the *Odyssey*, he used the newly invented Greek alphabet to write them down. The themes of his two poems evoke the period of the Mycenaean kingdoms, which existed five hundred years before his time. Drawing on oral tradition—the legends of his forebears and distant memories of a war in which Greece fought easterners from Asia Minor—he also mingled elements of contemporary life and history in his work. For example, while the *Iliad* describes the armor of Agamemnon's soldiers with an accuracy that has been

For centuries, historians, linguists, and geographers have been studying Homer's descriptions in an attempt to identify the places visited by Ulysses. Although their efforts have often been in vain, they have sometimes come up with plausible and reasonable suggestions. After the capture of Troy, Ulysses, king of Ithaca, set off for his island home, where the faithful Penelope and their son, Telemachus, were waiting for him. The voyage should only have taken a few weeks, but the malign actions of the gods and the ill-disposed elements made it ten years long! Ulysses was pursued by the wrath of the seagod Poseidon (brother of Zeus) after he blinded Poseidon's son, the fearsome Cyclops Polyphemus; but Ulysses was protected by Athena, goddess of wisdom and reason.

A CHILDHOOD DREAM

Heinrich Schliemann was born in 1822, son of a simple German pastor. From an early age he was fascinated by the stories of the destruction of Pompeii and the Trojan War. As his family could not afford to have him educated, at the age of fourteen he went to work for a grocer. Six years later he went to sea as a cabin boy and was shipwrecked. He was rescued but gave up the sea and took a humble job in a business in Amsterdam. He spent all his spare time studying foreign languages and quickly learned Dutch, English, French, Spanish, Italian, and Portuguese. Later he taught himself modern and ancient Greek and Arabic, with equal speed. He made a fortune in Russia trading in indigo, cotton, and tea, and he retired from business in 1866, able at last to devote himself to archaeology.

In 1869, carrying a copy of the Iliad, he traveled down the east coast of the Dardanelles and recognized the mound of Hissarlik as the site of ancient Troy. At that time, scholars were divided between this location and the village of Bunarbashi, farther south. In fact, there were no visible ruins in Bunarbashi or any fragments of remains underground, whereas some tentative digging had already been started at Hissarlik. Convinced that this was the right place, Schliemann began his own excavation in 1870, assisted by his young Greek wife,

Sophie. The digging went on until 1873, with a team of 100 to 150 laborers who uncovered the remains of the city ramparts and countless pottery and metal objects. The most exciting moment was on June 15, 1873, shortly before the site was due to close. Schliemann and his wife had entered a deep hole, when Schliemann saw something shining at the foot of a wall. "That is gold," he told Sophie. "Dismiss the workers, tell them it's my birthday and they can have the day off!" Then the two of them, using a knife, feverishly uncovered what they thought was a single object. But under their hands appeared treasure after treasure—diadems, earrings, rings, and gold and ivory plaques, which they wrapped in Sophie's shawl. Schliemann was convinced that it was the treasure of Priam, king of Troy, which the king or his servants saved when Troy was captured; either they must have hidden it before the city fell or it had been buried in the ruins of the palace. In fact, Schliemann had made an error of several centuries, just as he did with the treasure of Mycenae. But this is less important than the fact that he had proved his intuition right, and with his faith in the ancient texts and the magnitude of his discoveries, he aroused general enthusiasm and interest in archaeological excavation.

confirmed by archaeology, the *Odyssey* describes in part the Mediterranean as it was known in the eighth century B.C. The poet draws on ancient poetical and religious traditions but also incorporates the eyewitness descriptions of the sailors and merchants of his day. He speaks of the coasts and landscapes of the eastern Mediterranean from Crete to Italy, from Sicily to Egypt. The West, however, comes over in many instances as an unknown mysterious region, approaching the edges of the world. Homer, like all Greeks of his day and for centuries after, believed that the world consisted of a flat disc, ending perilously at the horizon.

This Roman mosaic, in the Bardo Museum in Tunis, shows the sirens trying to lure Ulysses and his companions with their songs.

TREASURES UNDER THE SEA

Its great square sail swelling in the wind, a ship left the Isle of Delos in the Aegean Sea for a long voyage toward the west, toward the sunset and the Pillars of Hercules.

In the Campania near Naples, the sailors completed the cargo with a load of black varnished pottery and then set sail again toward Massilia. But the ship never arrived. Within sight of the great port of Provincia Nostra, she was wrecked on the islet of the Grand Congloué, at the eastern point of the Isle de Riou. A navigational error? The result of a freak wind or sudden tempest? A badly stowed cargo? No one will ever know why this Roman ship foundered, with all souls on board, in the second century B.C.

The secrets of the amphorae

Like millions of other ships all over the Mediterranean, this one disappeared from history beneath the waves. And she would doubtless have remained there forever had not a deep-sea diver, two thousand years later, discovered her 165 feet down on the seabed. Between 1952 and 1961 the wreck was excavated by Commander Jacques Cousteau and the team of the *Calypso*, in collaboration with some archaeologists.

Over four hundred amphorae and seven thousand pieces of pottery were brought to the surface; close examination revealed their original contents, origin, and destination. This lengthy piece of work marked the true birth of underwater archaeology.

This was not the first wreck to be excavated in the Mediterranean. Between 1907 and 1913, off Mahdia in Tunisia, divers recovered bronzes and marbles from a wreck. But the purpose of that exercise was mainly to retrieve works of art, rather than to carry out a scientific excavation, for which the means were not available in those days. Today underwater archaeologists are able to study the site itself, analyze it, take measurements and photographs, and bring the findings to the surface in a scientific fashion. Underwater research has opened up our knowledge of the great trading routes of antiquity and of the goods that were bought and sold along the Mediterranean coastal regions. Contrary to what might be thought, some things survive quite well underwater. Silt, for example, is an excellent medium for preserving wrecks. In shallow water with a sandy or weedy bed, however, objects can be rendered unrecognizable through sedimentation, and the wood of hulls and decks can completely disintegrate.

Just as we give information on the labels of our canned foods today, useful data was painted on amphorae, and the data have often been preserved by burial at sea. This information includes the potter's seal, the weight of the amphora when empty and when full, the dealer's name, the name of the area where the contents were produced, and sometimes even the destination address. Obviously, historians can glean a great deal of knowledge from all this. And of course from the wrecks themselves they can learn a lot about the construction of ships. When a vessel sank, the heavy amphorae collected at the bottom of the hold, where they were buried in sand or silt, preserving the outline of the hull. From examining these remains, we also know that the Romans had three types of merchant vessels. The smallest were some 50 feet long, the medium-sized 72 feet, and the largest could be as long as 148 feet, holding up to five thousand amphorae. Dozens of oxcarts would have been needed to transport this kind of load overland. There was even a kind of tanker, in which enormous 6-foot jars, called *dolia*, were permanently fixed, for the transport of wine.

Many countries use small ships for archaeological research. In France, a former national marine craft, the Archeonaute, has been specially built to take aboard archaeologists, divers, and special equipment.

Before the discoveries made by underwater archaeology, all that was known about the ships of ancient times were the illustrations in reliefs and mosaics. This mosaic paved the Corporation Square of the Roman port of Ostia.

Underwater archaeology is a true scientific discipline. The site has to be found, and then exploratory dives have to be made to take measurements and photographs of the wreckage. Then, piece by piece, fragment by fragment, the precious finds are brought to the surface.

Modern-day pirates

These ships carried a great variety of cargoes. For example, a Roman wreck at Capo Testa in Sardinia was loaded with columns, iron bars, and lead ingots; another, in the Hyères Islands, contained tin ingots and several tons of iron bars; a third, off Corsica, was carrying oil, wine, and pickling brine; yet another, in the outer harbor of Carry-le-Rouet in the west of Provence, contained cut stones destined for building the ramparts of Massilia in the Hellenistic period.

Most wrecks date from the Roman Empire, but sometimes archaeologists make discoveries from earlier times. Off the Turkish coast of Asia Minor near Cape Gelidonya, a wreck was found from the thirteenth century B.C., loaded with bronze, copper, and tin ingots. Other similar ships from the Bronze Age have been discovered, one near Haborium on the coast of Israel, the other in the Bay of Lipari in Italy. By examining all these ancient ships, researchers have found out how the hull, deck, and steering oars were made, and what kinds of wood were used. But we still don't know everything about the rigging, sails, and fittings.

It is rare to find what are normally thought of as treasures, like silver and gold. But in 1980 some French divers did recover some very beautiful furniture from a wreck in Golfe Juan, including bronze-plated beds with carved decorations. This ship has been dated from the first century B.C., and its cargo was undoubtedly manufactured in the workshop of a Greek bronzesmith. But the archaeologists have only been able to recover a small part of it, for the wreck had already been pillaged by other divers. Indeed, looting has become the greatest enemy of underwater archaeology. There are some veritable gangs, highly organized and well equipped, who scour the Mediterranean for amphorae, ceramics, bronzes, and marbles to supply a network of European and American antique dealers. The countries around the Mediterranean are virtually powerless against this traffic, and although it is destroying an irreplaceable heritage, legislation does not properly deal with it.

The statues of Riace

One of the most remarkable discoveries was made on August 16, 1972, by an Italian diver exploring along the east coast of Calabria. On that day, diving 980 feet off the shore of the Riace Marina, he caught sight of the shoulder of a bronze statue emerging from the sand. As he tried to free it, he was even more surprised to find a second statue alongside the first, similar in size and also amazingly intact. These two works of art, exhumed from their submarine grave, were taken to a laboratory in Florence to be cleaned, analyzed, and treated. They represent naked warriors, one 5 feet 11 inches tall and the other 6 feet 6 inches tall. They were made in Greece in the fifth century B.C., in the style known as "Severe," of Attic influence and perhaps origin. The statues are among the extremely rare examples of the work of the master bronzesmiths in the century of Pericles. The only comparable works of this period are the *Auriga* ("Charioteer") found at Delphi and the *Zeus* (or possibly *Poseidon*) also recovered from the bottom of the sea on the north coast of the Isle of Euboea, and now in the Athens Museum.

A collection of amphorae in the hold of a Roman ship. Two thousand years ago they were used to transport wine.

MARBLE AND BRONZE

In antiquity, all forms of art were used for religious purposes. Temples and statues had to proclaim the glory of the gods and the pride of the cities, who competed in building ever more sumptuous and dazzling monuments.

The beauty of marble

Sculptors were employed by architects to decorate friezes and pediments; worshipers paid them to ornament shrines as offerings, and they carved reliefs to beautify tombs. All over Greece the sculptors knew, copied, admired, and criticized the works of their rivals. The most famous, Phidias, decorated the Parthenon in the fifth century B.C. with the famous frieze of the Panathenaic Festival; he also created the chryselephantine (gold and ivory) statues of Athena and Zeus at Olympia. After him, the most important names to survive are Praxiteles, the first person to sculpt goddesses in the nude, and Lysippus, who sculpted a portrait of Alexander the Great.

As with architecture, the material most often used by sculptors was the marble that abounded in the Aegean Islands, at Paros, Naxos, and Thasos, and on the mainland at Ephesus in Asia Minor. In addition to its fine grain, color, and extreme durability, marble is an exceptionally beautiful material. The most famous and favorite type came from Paros. Light can pass through a piece of Parian marble 1 ½ inches thick, and the Greeks called it "that which lights."

Most Greek sculptors also created masterpieces in bronze; they liked its color and the patina it acquired over time. The first stage in making a bronze statue was to make a small-scale model. From this, a wooden carving was made the actual size of the projected statue. Then there was a choice of two possible techniques. The oldest consisted of applying a sheet of bronze over the wooden carving. The second was the technique called "lost wax." The sculptor prepared a clay core in the shape of the statue, covered that with a layer of wax, and then placed that in a second mold. Molten bronze, an alloy of copper and tin, was poured into the space occupied by the wax, and the wax melted and drained away through prepared holes. The mold was allowed to cool. It was then broken, and the bronze sculpture was taken out.

The Riace bronzes.
These superb bronze statues, discovered off Calabria in 1972, were cast in 460 B.C. by Greek bronzesmiths.

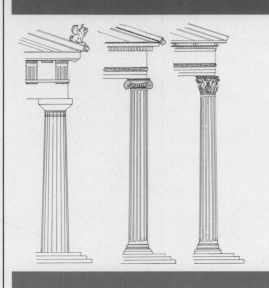

The architects of antiquity used several styles in building and decorating temples and monuments. The Doric style evolved from early timber buildings. The column rests directly on the steps, and the capital consists of a kind of circular pad and a square block. In the Ionic style, the base of the column is molded, and the capital is characterized by spiral scrolls, called volutes. In the Corinthian style the capitals are decorated with acanthus leaves.

Paintings and mosaics

Roman artists imitated the Greeks in both marble and bronze sculpture, but they also developed original techniques and styles in other areas. They were excellent painters, an art practiced and appreciated by all social classes. Small shopkeepers and artisans often ordered frescoes in honor of a deity or to advertise their wares. Nobles and landowners got painters to decorate their country villas, as did the wealthy middle-class townspeople. The themes of Roman paintings developed through the

The outstandingly high quality of Greek pottery is due to the minute attention the potters paid to every stage of manufacture. The clay was chosen with care and then soaked for a long time in water to rid it of impurities. Then it was shaped on a potter's wheel; plates and wide-necked vases were made in one piece, while vases with narrow necks and complicated shapes were made in several pieces and soldered together. The craftworkers were so skilled that they were able to make vases only 2 millimeters thick. When the pot was the desired shape, its sides were decorated with landscapes or people, using a brush and various colored pigments. It was fired in a small brick kiln using different types of fuel—dry wood, green wood, and damp sawdust. In the sixth century B.C. Athenian "black-figure" pottery (above left) spread throughout the Greek world. In the following century came the "red-figure" period (above right). In the Roman period, particularly in the Arezzo region of Italy and at Lezoux and La Graufesenque in Gaul, pottery was produced with the decorations molded in relief. This kind of pottery was easier, quicker, and less expensive to make, and it totally supplanted painted pottery; however, painted Greek vases remain unsurpassed for their illustrations of mythological stories and their thousands of scenes of everyday life.

Republican and Imperial eras. Some wall paintings imitated architectural features, sometimes in the *trompe l'oeil* technique, which made them look almost real; others showed lively scenes, characters, landscapes, and gardens. This form of interior decoration was the usual practice in Roman houses and was carried out by craftworkers attached to the building trade. These painters were often slaves performing what was regarded as manual labor, which would have been beneath free citizens. But some painters were famous and respected. They painted small easel paintings for rich clients or wooden panels to be put up in public buildings.

The Romans adopted the art of mosaic from the Greeks; the remains of mosaics can be found all over the empire, especially in North Africa. Building up pictures out of small stone cubes set in a cement base, Roman mosaic artists could produce very large and elaborate compositions to decorate walls and floors. Their remains are among the most valuable evidence that we have for obtaining a picture of the life, beliefs, and customs of the Roman Empire.

CHRONOLOGY

2900   Founding of the Phoenician port of Byblos.

2000   First palaces built in Crete.

1500   Minoan civilization at its peak. Cuneiform alphabet used in Ugarit, Syria. Growth of Mycenaean cities.

1400   End of Minoan power.

1200   Iron used in the eastern Mediterranean. Decline of Mycenaean power. The "sea people" from Asia Minor migrate toward Egypt.

1000   Alphabet used by the Phoenicians.

800   Development of the Greek alphabet from the Phoenician. Founding of Carthage. Hut settlements on the hills of Rome.

776   First recorded Olympian Games. Start of the Greek calendar.

760–650   Development of Etruscan towns. Greek colonies in southern Italy and Sicily.

753   Traditional date of founding of Rome by Romulus.

600   Confederation of twelve Etruscan cities. At the command of Pharaoh Necho, Phoenician navigators sail around Africa.

640–560   Life of Solon, Greek legislator and poet, founder of democracy.

509   The last Etruscan king driven from Rome. Founding of the Roman Republic.

490   First war between Greeks and Persians. The Greeks win the battle of Marathon.

525–456   Life of Aeschylus, the first great Greek dramatist.

457   Building of the long walls linking Athens to the port of Piraeus.

447–432   Building of the Parthenon by Ictinus (architect) and Phidias (sculptor) at the command of Pericles.

485–425   Life of Herodotus, first great historian of antiquity.

427–347   Life of Plato, one of the greatest Greek philosophers.

431–404   The Peloponnesian War brings an end to Athenian power.

390   The Gauls sack Rome and besiege the Capitol.

336   Death of Philip II of Macedonia. Alexander becomes king at the age of 20.

334   Alexander lands in Asia Minor.

384–322   Life of the scholar and philosopher Aristotle.

323   Death of Alexander in Babylon.

282   After defeating the Samnites, Etruscans, and Celts, Rome controls central and northern Italy.

263–241   First Punic War

287–212   Life of the scholar Archimedes.

218–201   Second Punic War; Hannibal invades Italy.

149–146   Third Punic War; destruction of Carthage.

133–121   Greek social reforms.

73–71   Slaves' rebellion led by the gladiator Spartacus.

58–51   Julius Caesar's conquest of Gaul.

44   Assassination of Caesar.

27–14   Reign of Augustus.

79   Eruption of Vesuvius, burying Herculaneum and Pompeii.

70–80   Building of the Colosseum.

98–117   Reign of Trajan.

220   Emperor Caracalla grants Roman citizenship to all free men in the empire.

250–300   Germanic tribes make their first raids into the Roman Empire.

306–337   Reign of Constantine. Recognition of Christianity (313). Byzantium becomes capital of the Roman Empire.

395   The empire divided into Eastern Empire and Western Empire.

410   The Visigoths, led by Alaric, capture and pillage Rome.

476   Romulus Augustulus, last emperor of the Western Empire, deposed by the Germanic Odoacer.

527–565   Reign of Justinian, emperor of Eastern Empire.

INDEX

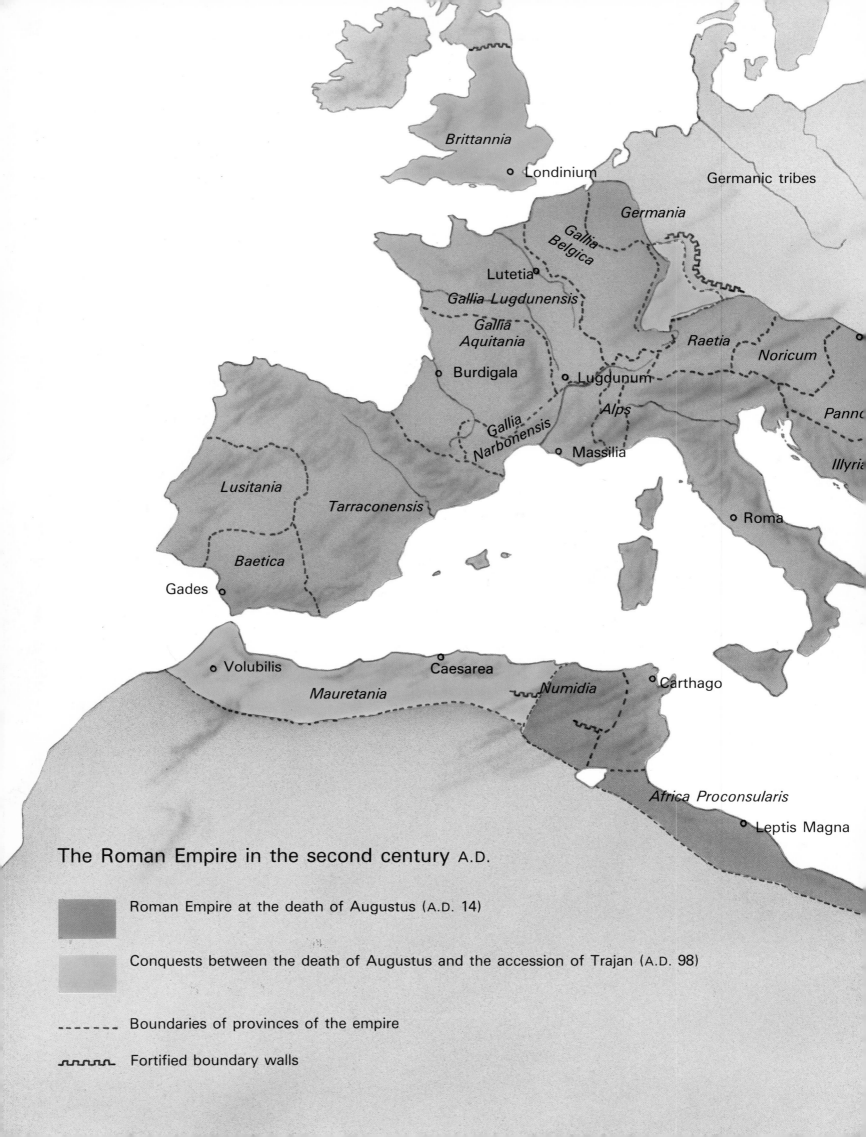

Brittannia

○ Londinium

Germanic tribes

Germania

Gallia Belgica

Lutetia ○

Gallia Lugdunensis

Gallia Aquitania

○ Burdigala

○ Lugdunum

Raetia

Noricum

Alps

Pann...

Gallia Narbonensis

○ Massilia

Illyria

Lusitania

Tarraconensis

○ Roma

Baetica

Gades ○

○ Volubilis

○ Caesarea

○ Carthago

Numidia

Mauretania

Africa Proconsularis

○ Leptis Magna

The Roman Empire in the second century A.D.

Roman Empire at the death of Augustus (A.D. 14)

Conquests between the death of Augustus and the accession of Trajan (A.D. 98)

- - - - - Boundaries of provinces of the empire

ᴖᴖᴖᴖᴖ Fortified boundary walls